HOW KIND PEOPLE GET TOUGH

How Kind People Get Tough

Assertiveness Tools, Tips, and Techniques for More Confidence and Happier Relationships

Marléne Rose Shaw

Published by Power of Love Books

POWER OF LOVE
BOOKS

ISBN Number: 978-0-9935419-1-9

Editor: Lois Rose
Illustrator: Jamie Shaw
Typesetting: Ryan Ashcroft

Risk Assessment Note

The tools tips and techniques in this book are effective ways to be more assertive within the context of a non-abusive relationship. If you think you may be in an abusive relationship, possibly even in physical danger, I recommend you seek support.

Sadly, for whatever reason, some people lack self-awareness and are simply unable to take responsibility for their actions. Trying to change them by applying the techniques in this book may make matters worse. Please remember that it is not your responsibility to try to change others; rather it is your responsibility to take care of yourself. Seek out a professional who is trained to help, and speak to your family and friends. The more people you have to support you the better.

To all my clients

Thank you for all

you have taught me

Acknowledgements

Special Gratitude to

Lois Rose: a wonderful editor

Jamie Shaw: for his outstanding artwork

Contents

More Than Just A Book

This book is more than just a book. It is a process for change. It incorporates practical tools and techniques which have been used to help thousands of people change their lives for the better.

It also contains a free online companion course for you at:

www.howkindpeople.com

The course is in two parts:

- Worksheets and Guides
- Intentional Life Plan

Worksheets and Guides

Here you will find a range of resources which includes video, worksheets, checklists, and exercises based on the book content. It will help you put the tools, tips, and techniques into practice.

Intentional Life Plan

This part contains your **Intentional Life Plan**. You'll find templates to help you complete your plan, which is described in Part Three of the book. Once completed, your plan will serve as a guide for you to refer back to in different scenarios and situations in your life where being more assertive can help. It will help you find clarity, set good boundaries, and be more intentional.

Your **Intentional Life Plan** will give you:

- A very clear vision of what your new life will look like
- A guide for how you're going to make that happen easily and effectively, such as communication skills you will use and boundaries you will set
- A reference point to refer to in challenging situations.

I encourage you to take advantage of this online companion course for two good reasons.

1. I've created the resources specifically to help you take the tools, tips, and techniques referred to in this book and apply them to your own personal circumstances.
2. Taking action in this way means you'll be training yourself to help you think and behave in ways that are very beneficial to your confidence, and your relationships.

Quick Wins

Throughout the book you will also occasionally see the thumbs up icon to denote something you can do to create a quick win, such as a communication tip or assertiveness strategy. You may also like to use these tips to inspire you when filling out your **Intentional Life Plan.**

Introduction

As I sit here on my balcony, the evening sunlight casts its golden glow across the rooftops. The swifts, swooping and gliding, claim the sky with confidence. As is their right.

I smile as I recall a client saying to me this morning, 'If only I had half as much confidence as you. How did you get to be like that?'

She was right; I am a confident person. Now.

For many years I had very low self-esteem—I saw myself as far less worthy than others. It seems strange to me now that I didn't even question that. I guess on some level I believed that I didn't deserve any better.

In those days, I was always looking to others to validate me. Which meant, of course, that I always ended up feeling let down because I'd set them up with an impossible task—I was making them responsible for my own happiness.

I often attached myself to the wrong people—people who really weren't equipped to offer me the sort of respect and regard that I now know I deserved. I didn't plan for the future because to me life was just about surviving each day. Nor did I see myself as anyone who could expect to have a career or be successful in life. That was for other people—those *confident* people.

As I look back on that powerless young woman, I understand that my lack of self-worth and unhelpful beliefs had been passed down to me through generations of people who had experienced their own fears and insecurities.

Those people were not privileged to be born into a world where personal development and psychology were deemed to be of importance. They had little awareness of self, how relationships work, or of the harm they were causing by passing on trauma from generation to generation.

Helping clients over many years has shown me that this is not uncommon. Most can trace back generations of trauma: patterns unwittingly passed down through time.

I feel so lucky to have arrived in this world at a time where breaking these patterns is possible. I know that what has helped me to become the self-assured and confident woman I am today are the therapeutic studies I've been privileged to undertake, and putting those skills to work in my therapy practice.

My clients have also been my delightful teachers. In all the learning, training, practising, and experience of helping them step into their light, I too have been able to step into mine. I am so grateful to them.

The Topic of Confidence is Never Far Away

In a way, this book has been steadily writing itself for years, because it's based on the very work that my clients and I have done. And during all this time, the topic of confidence has never been far away in our sessions—either looking us straight in the face or hovering somewhere in the background.

Whether I'm helping someone with a relationship problem, with their confidence, or with overcoming anger or anxiety, at some point they will almost certainly talk about wanting to become more assertive.

Becoming more assertive is something many people aspire to, yet they're confused about what that really means. They tell me, 'I don't want to come across as arrogant—I don't want to be unkind.' So they've learnt to use other ways to manage the challenges in their relationships.

In a bid to avoid criticism and rejection, they put on a mask and they put on an act. They people-please, they allow others to get away with poor behaviour, they say yes when they want to say no and, amidst all that, they forget their own worth.

We all do this to a certain extent.

Yet there comes a time in life when we become tired of the act. We begin to see that all this people-pleasing and trying to prove ourselves simply takes us around in circles, never truly resolving the problems in our relationships.

At this stage, the idea of continuing through life *not* being our authentic true self begins to feel heavy and burdensome. It becomes far less appealing to stay in that comfort zone than to sum up the courage to step into the light and speak our truth.

What we all want is to know that who we are and what we feel matters. We want others to validate us as worthy of regard and respect.

We want to be able to speak up, say what we really think and what we really want, without fear of criticism. We want to be heard and responded to in ways that show us others acknowledge us as significant.

We want all our relationships—with our spouse, family, friends or colleagues—to be happy and to feel secure, and for those relationships to be an inspiring context to learn and grow into our wisdom.

Why This Book Will Help You

Becoming more assertive isn't just one single 'thing'. It is a process of combining self-awareness and insight, learning specific tools and techniques, and taking small, actionable steps to build confidence. This is the journey that my clients take through therapy. I have written this book so that I can take you on a similar journey.

Just like the many people I've helped over the years, it's very likely that you're here with me now because the time is right for you. You're ready to move on to the next level, and step into a new, more self-assured version of yourself.

As you learn to be more assertive, you'll find that your confidence soars. You'll let go of old fears and confusion. You'll be clear about where you stand, what you want from life and certain about how to make that happen.

Not only will you feel more secure in your relationships—they'll become more meaningful and inspiring. Not only will you begin to improve the relationship you have with yourself—you'll begin to truly love yourself. You'll start to lead the exceptional life that is your right.

Understanding

Part One

Can Kind People Be Tough?

Chapter 1
Who Are the Kind People?

If I were to ask what kindness means for you, I'm guessing you'd tell me that it's about making another person feel good by offering them care, consideration, and compassion. I'm sure most people would agree with you, and I would say that it is all these things—and more.

Over the years, I've been privileged to meet so many inspiring people; they've come into my therapy room and shared their stories with me; they've told me about their dreams and their desires, their worries, and their fears. They've told me about the intricacies of their relationships, and in those discussions, the subject of kindness comes up.

People don't actually tell me that they want to be kinder. What they do say is that they want to be more assertive, but they worry that that will make them *un*kind. Their kindness is a sort of given; there's an assumption that it's already there within them—they just don't want to lose it in their efforts to be more assertive in their relationships.

Kindness is supremely important to human happiness; it has a special energy. We all enjoy the feel of it. Simply talking about kindness with a client always puts a smile on our faces—it's as though a special quality has come into the room by the mere mention of the word.

But what exactly is this intangible energy that feels so good? That question can be more clearly answered when we consider: Why do people actually *want* kindness in their lives?

You see, while kindness manifests itself in all these lovely ways, such as care, consideration, and compassion, at its heart, kindness really means connection. Whether it's helping someone out, inspiring them, being compassionate, or even simply giving them a smile—these acts of kindness are always about connection in some form. So, when we offer kindness to someone, we're saying, 'I'm here with you; we are connected; you are not alone; we are together.'

It is this connection through kindness that is fundamental to humanity's survival. Michael J. Chase, bestselling author, renowned speaker, and one of today's most influential voices for creating a kinder world, says: 'The only way that we're going to change the world is to change ourselves—world peace must develop out of inner peace. It all comes down to every single one of us: seven billion people making the decision, getting up every day, and saying, "How can I be kinder, how can I open my heart? How can I make the world a more beautiful, loving and kind place?"'

So given that kindness can be such a powerful force in our lives, it's a wonder that we don't all go around in a constant state of bliss and harmony, having amazing relationships. But we don't.

We're certainly not continuously performing kind acts towards each other, or even to ourselves, and we're not always thinking kind thoughts either. It's not surprising. Navigating the relationships of our lives can be complicated. We each have our own ideas about how we want our life to be, and the others around us have their ideas about how they want their lives to be. The next thing we know, we're clashing with those others because there's such a muddle of emotions, miscommunication and misunderstandings.

The problem is that we can all get distracted. If we're stressed about some issue, for example, we're so preoccupied with solving that issue, that thoughts of kindness don't even enter our heads. Stress puts people into survival mode, and in that mode, the most important thing is to solve the problem. So our focus is purely on finding a solution—nothing else. It means that we can sometimes even be *un*kind to each other—not because we don't care, but because our attention is elsewhere.

London, Circa 1980s

Many years ago when I was a teenager, I was on a tube train

in London. I was in a great hurry to reach Euston Station, because I knew I'd have to dash across the concourse and catch the mainline train to Glasgow. I wasn't sure I was going to make it in time. I really *had* to catch that train!

The tube was packed as usual—there were no free seats, so I had to stand, supporting myself by hanging onto one of the straps. We pulled into Euston. The doors opened. Then, it all happened.

There was a man in glasses standing next to me, and as I let go of the strap, my arm brushed against the side of his face, caught his glasses and somehow or other catapulted his glasses down into the gap between the tube train and the platform—down onto the rail line!

I was absolutely mortified. A shy teenager at the time, with very little confidence, I just didn't know how to handle the situation.

I remember saying to the man:

'It's OK, the station staff will help you, I have to dash,' and off I went!

All these years later, I still feel guilty about just leaving him there.

My lack of kindness that day wasn't because I knocked that poor man's glasses down onto the rails—that was an accident.

My lack of kindness was due to the fact that I abandoned him. Instead of saying, 'It'll be OK, I'll stay and help,' I just left him there alone. I disconnected from him. And that was not kind.

But even then, back in those teen years, where altruism wasn't top of my list of priorities, I was still in general someone who desired to be kind. My behaviour that day was the contrary of kindness because I was stressed. I simply made a mistake.

The Goodies and the Baddies

When someone is unkind, it can be hard to contemplate that they've simply made a mistake. It's hard to grasp this because human beings are so quick to judge each other. We witness someone's behaviour and assign them a category of good, well-meaning, and likeable, or bad, uncaring, and selfish.

This labelling of people begins very early on in life, where parents and teachers say things like 'Good girl. Good boy' or 'You're bad. You're naughty', and so on. The idea is then further reinforced in children's books, films, and games, where the characters are branded as the *goodies* or the *baddies.*

Of course, as we grow up, we begin to understand that people are much more complex than this. However, those long-ago messages received in childhood have already created a belief system: a powerful subconscious programme that tells us that there are the 'good people' and there are the 'bad people'.

This is the reason that so many people struggle with the concept of being kind *and* assertive at the same time. They have formed a mistaken notion that assertiveness is a negative thing. 'I want to be more assertive,' my clients tell me, 'but won't that make me mean?'

This idea that kindness is a good thing and assertiveness is not, is a common myth. As we move forward through this book, you'll see that being assertive is not that negative, bad thing that so many people fear. In fact, when applied effectively, kindness and assertiveness are quite akin to each other. And as we understand this fully, we're able to embrace assertiveness—see it in a positive light—and begin to have more confident and self-assured relationships.

The Desire to be Kind

Now I can almost hear you thinking, 'Yes, but there are some people who are just basically nasty.' I agree: there are people who consistently treat others poorly, and there's no excuse for that. The point I'm making is that I doubt those people start their day with the thought: 'Now how can I be unkind today?'

It's likely that they're simply trying to overcome some pain, real or perceived, and so they feel justified by their unwise behaviour. They don't classify it as unkindness; in fact, they may be quite taken aback by the idea that they're being unkind.

To categorise ourselves, and others, as unkind then, doesn't do us any favours because it keeps us stuck in a role. The reality is that there are rarely any total *goodies* or *baddies* here: most of us are kind people in the very fact that we value kindness as a quality that we want to have in our lives.

So, when I refer to *the kind people* in this book, I'm not referring to some special sub-section of people who have this thing called kindness, whilst others don't. I'm talking about those of us who have a desire to be kind, to be caring, and connect with others in good and healthy and happy ways. That desire is pretty much in all of us. I guess, then, that we each are *one of the kind people.*

The question is though, can kind people get tough? How do we learn to be assertive, get our needs met, speak up, and set effective boundaries whilst remaining kind?

Chapter 2
Can Kind People Be Tough?

I've helped many people become more confident and have better, happier relationships, and, as I mentioned earlier, many of those people have told me that they'd like to be more assertive. Yet, even as they say this, the hesitancy in their voice and their slightly doubtful expression signal to me that they think wanting to be more assertive is a bad thing. People worry that in being assertive, they'll be pushy and arrogant— heart-*less* rather than heart-*centred.*

This confusion often arises when people think that becoming more assertive involves simply learning techniques—practical skills that they can use in given situations. It's certainly true that there are some very effective techniques (you'll find several in this book), but first we must get out of the head and into the heart—because this is where true assertiveness begins. Get this bit right and those techniques will be much more effective.

I have found that people can begin to connect with their heart by digging a little deeper, exploring what they actually want from leading a more assertive life. This simple act alone means they're becoming more self-assured.

People want to be acknowledged, valued, and respected. They want to be able to speak up, be heard, and get their needs met. They want to feel comfortable in their own skin, and accepted as they are. And interestingly, it's often in these early exploratory conversations that my clients begin to see that leading a more confident life is just as much about how they treat themselves, as it is about how others treat them.

The Quiet Voice in Your Heart

We all have moments in our lives when being a bit bolder would be a good idea. It could be something that happens in a relationship: with a spouse, a friend, or maybe with a colleague.

Sometimes, it's very obvious that being more assertive is called for. If someone has been abusive towards you, for example, well, that's clear! *(I just want to pause here to say that if you think you may be in an abusive situation, do read the Risk Assessment note at the beginning of this book.)*

Then at other times things are not so clear. Maybe you say yes, because you're not sure how to say no, and then later you regret it and feel resentful of having to give away your time or energy. Maybe you don't speak up when someone disrespects you because you're not sure who's right or wrong, or where you stand in a situation. Maybe it just seems easier to go along with things to keep the peace.

We've all been there.

But there will always be a vague sense of discomfort. This is the quiet voice in your heart. 'This isn't right,' it whispers, gently. 'You deserve better.'

This voice in your heart is the voice of love. It will tell you the truth when you're not being loving towards yourself, and it will guide you in how to truly love others.

If we could each of us listen to our own inner voice, and act on it with courage, life would be so much simpler. The problem is that so many of us find that hard to do.

And there's a reason for that. There are some innate blocks—fundamental aspects of human conditioning—that cause us to feel fearful and can make stepping into the light and speaking our authentic truth a challenge.

We'll be exploring these blocks as we move through the book, and I'll be teaching you how to let them go and how to practise being more assertive in effective and confident ways. We'll be exploring all this via various scenarios with lots of examples and case studies. But for now, let's take a deeper look at what true assertiveness is.

In many years of helping people, I've discovered that assertiveness is:

- Leading an Intentional Life
- Being Authentic
- Finding Courage to be Vulnerable
- Focusing on Love
- Feeling Gratitude
- Seeking a Win-Win Outcome

Leading an Intentional Life

I've noticed that people make the mistake of thinking that being assertive means reacting to how others have behaved towards them. Reactions though, are random: they're not planned. There's nothing to be gained from drifting through life with no clear idea of who we are, or how we want our relationships to be. Doing that is handing responsibility for our own happiness over to others, and then getting upset when we don't like their behaviour.

We can't control other people, or events. What we can most certainly do, however, is create some guidelines on how we want life to be for ourselves. We can then use those guidelines as a framework from which to respond to those people and events. When we are intentional in this way, we're taking responsibility for our own happiness. That is true assertiveness.

Being Authentic

We all wear the people-pleasing mask from time to time—some more than others. We hide behind the mask, smiling, keeping everyone happy, or saying nothing, even though we may be feeling devalued and disrespected by someone's behaviour. In the moment, it seems easier to ignore the inner voice which urges us to speak up. Later though, we feel bad because deep down we know we weren't really being true to ourselves.

Authenticity is an integral part of leading an assertive life. It means listening to that inner voice and acting on what we hear. It means stepping into the light and saying, 'This is me; this is my value. I'd like you to treat me in accordance with that. I intend to treat you, and myself, in accordance with that too!'

Many people have told me that they want to speak up and be more authentic in their relationships, but they worry that in doing so they'll cause more trouble. It certainly can feel very risky to challenge disrespect.

But hiding behind a mask is not the answer. When we're not authentic, we keep a distance between ourselves and others, and that means we miss out on the close connections that we could have.

The solution is to learn how to be authentic in ways that feel less risky. And given that assertiveness is just as much about the relationship you have with yourself, you can make it feel less risky by learning to be authentic with yourself first. You can do this by having an inner dialogue with yourself, listening to your feelings, and acknowledging when something isn't right. Ask yourself questions, such as 'What is my worth here? How do I want to treat myself and have others treat me?'

Remember, this is your own private conversation—nobody has to know about it. However, the very act of asking yourself these questions will help you feel more self-aware—you'll naturally feel more confident.

Finding the Courage to be Vulnerable

People are often surprised at the idea that being assertive can mean being vulnerable, because in their mind they see assertiveness as the opposite of vulnerability. There's a general image of the assertive person as someone who goes around, head held high: nothing phases them. Because of this mistaken idea, people seem almost ashamed of feeling vulnerable. It's as if they believe they should be constantly wearing a superhero cape, never allowing themselves to be, well, simply human.

But we *are* human, with all our strengths, our weaknesses, and all the bits in between—and that's OK.

While it may sound contradictory, the more we allow ourselves to be vulnerable, the more we can gain confidence. This is because when we allow ourselves to be vulnerable, we're saying, 'This is me and I accept me as I am, right now in this moment.'

Self-acceptance is a powerful foundation for confidence. Once we open our hearts and accept ourselves, others accept us too. They respect and admire our courage in being our true selves, and that validation is a great boost for self-esteem.

And, we are back to connection here. People will often embrace someone else's vulnerability because it signals to them that they too, can be vulnerable. Vulnerability, then, connects us in our humanity; it draws us closer to each other. With connection comes a sense of support and that too brings confidence. Counterintuitive as it may seem, finding the courage to be vulnerable is one important aspect of leading an assertive life.

Focusing on Love

I talk a lot about love and fear in my work. Much of how we are in life— what we think, how we feel, and even what drives our behaviour—comes from either a state of love or a state of fear.

And I've found people often place assertiveness in the fear category instead of the love category. They think that they must retaliate for having been disempowered in some way by tilting the balance of power back in favour of themselves—by being forceful or by getting others to behave in a certain way. But isn't that just shifting the fear from one person to another? That can feel very heavy and burdensome. No wonder people struggle with it!

I've also seen that people tend to think of assertiveness as some type of outside force—something that they must discover, acquire, and then utilise. The reality is that finding ways to be more assertive comes from an *inside* force. And that inside force is the power of love. It is an inner strength. When you love yourself and become absolutely real with yourself and, when you are authentic about who you are and what you want, you'll find such a sense of empowerment. Then, the ability to gain respect and feel in control of your own life will happen in a very natural way. It's not something you have to *do*, but rather something that you can *align with*.

Feeling Gratitude

Another way to embrace assertiveness as a loving way of being is to see it in terms of gratitude for life. Life is a gift in itself. When we seek to be more confident and self-assured, we're appreciating that gift—we're consciously acknowledging our own worthiness and value, saying: 'Thank you. Thank you for giving me this precious life! I'm going to live it fully and honestly. I'm going to be the real me, rather than being a version of myself that others expect me to be. I'm going to let others know my value by asking them to honour it, and I'm going to treat myself, and them, with respect.'

Seeking a Win-Win Outcome

When people come for help with their confidence, they often tell me:

'I find I compare myself to others: I'm always rating myself as better, or worse, than them.'

As I mentioned earlier, human beings are judgemental by nature; we're prone to making comparisons and putting each other into categories. When we do this, we can't help but create an imbalance of power, because one person is deemed to be better than the other.

Dr Thomas A. Harris, psychiatrist, wrote a bestseller called *I'm OK – You're OK*, based upon the ideas of Transactional Analysis by Dr Eric Berne. It demonstrates this power imbalance clearly. In this model we see four life positions which have a profound impact on how a person experiences their relationships. They are:

- I'm Not OK, You're OK
- I'm Not OK, You're Not OK
- I'm OK, You're Not OK
- I'm OK, You're OK

I'm Not OK, You're OK

In this position, the person sees themselves as the less worthy one in their relationships. A person who holds this position will often, unconsciously, accept mistreatment from others, not realising they deserve better.

I'm Not OK, You're Not OK

This is the least desirable position to be in. It means that a person lacks self-worth and regards others as unworthy too.

I'm OK, You're Not OK

In this position, a person feels good about themselves, but they see others as less worthy and with little potential.

I'm OK, You're OK

This is the optimum position. It means that a person feels

good about themselves, and they feel good about others too. They feel competent and they see others as potentially competent.

Because we *all* want to feel worthy and lovable, it's helpful to understand that true assertiveness isn't about winning or losing; it's about looking at everyone in a given situation and finding a winning outcome for all concerned. Aiming for **I'm OK, You're OK** means we're onto a good thing because it will always draw people towards us rather than push them away. One way to reach this position is to ask ourselves the simple question, 'How can I find a balance of love and empowerment for everyone in this situation?'

So, can kind people be tough? Well, most certainly they can! Any of us can learn to be more assertive, whilst remaining the kind and caring person we've always been, because the more we explore, the more we see that kindness and assertiveness are really not so far apart after all.

As we saw in chapter 1 'Who are the Kind People', kindness, at its core, is all about connection and love. It's a way of communicating 'I am here with you—you are not alone.' It comes from the heart.

And, when we consider the true meaning of leading an authentic life: being open, sharing vulnerability, and seeking loving outcomes for all, we see that this, too, is about connection and love. It also comes from the heart. If kindness and assertiveness share these same essential qualities, it would seem clear that we can indeed be kind and assertive all at the same time.

But there's another piece to the *kindness plus assertiveness* puzzle. The answer lies in being the right *kind* of kind.

Chapter 3

What *Kind* of Kind are You Being?

In chapter 1 'Who Are the Kind People?', we saw that the kind people I refer to in this book are pretty much all of us, and that includes you. Even though you may make mistakes, and sometimes cause yourself and others difficulties, it's unlikely that you do these things with any real intention of doing harm. In your heart you're generally a well-meaning person, and that's what makes you one of the kind people.

As we've seen, kindness is all about love and connection. We've also seen that assertiveness is about love and connection too. It seems clear then that it's perfectly possible for any of us to be both kind and assertive at the same time.

There is one small difference though. Kindness says, 'I'm here with you, offering connection: we are together.' Assertiveness says, 'I want to be here with you, offering connection, and let's do it together, in the best possible way.' The thing to notice here is *in the best possible way.*

In order to be kind plus assertive then, we need to think in terms of being kind in the best possible way. That is, we need to make sure we're being the right *kind* of kind.

You see, while we may have the desire to be kind, we sometimes get kindness all muddled up. We can think we're being kind when actually we're not being kind at all. If you're keeping someone happy to the point that you're denying your own worth—is that being kind to you, and ultimately to them? If you keep giving in because someone keeps asking, and you don't want to say no—is that being kind to you, and ultimately to them?

Sam, 21

Sam's girlfriend, Fay, was feeling very low. Having completed her degree three months previously, she still couldn't find a decent job. Sam felt sorry for Fay; he knew what it was like to be unemployed and broke.

Every day, Fay would lie on the sofa, watching TV, smoking, and scoffing junk food. The house was a mess; she did nothing to contribute, and if Sam tried to say anything, she'd get moody and snap at him.

Sam could see that Fay's confidence had taken a knock and he wanted to be kind. So he put up with her moods and her laziness. As time passed, though, he was getting fed up with it all—he was beginning to feel resentful.

Was Sam being kind to Fay?

In our desire to be kind and caring, we can find ourselves putting up with disrespect, and then feeling confused and resentful.

Sam loved Fay and wanted to make her happy, but he didn't know what to do. His emotions vacillated from resentment to compassion, from irritability to concern.

When our emotions take over, it can be difficult to think straight and decide how to handle a situation. However, there is a way to step back, see the clearer picture, and navigate your way out of the confusion. And that way is to ask yourself:

'What *kind* of kind am I being?'

Misguided Kindness or Conscious Kindness?

Understanding the difference between misguided kindness and conscious kindness is the key to having more confident and successful relationships of all types.

In later chapters, I'll be sharing a number of case studies with you and providing methods on how to be assertive in different situations and scenarios. As we explore them, I'll often be referring to Misguided Kindness and Conscious Kindness. So let's begin by getting clearer on what these mean and how they differ.

Misguided Kindness

Sam was misguided in his laid-back response to Fay. He wasn't really helping her at all. He certainly wasn't being authentic by hiding how he felt about her moods and her laziness. Her behaviour was disrespectful to him, and to their relationship. His attempts at trying to mollify her actually meant the relationship was off balance. He had put himself squarely in the position of I'm not OK, You're OK.

In reality, misguided kindness isn't kindness at all—it's really just fear disguised as kindness. It's an illusion of kindness that shows up in ways that seem like an easy solution at the time.

I've been there myself, and maybe you too will have recognised misguided kindness in your own relationships as you read about Sam's situation. Perhaps you've gone into people-pleasing mode or made yourself available (when you really weren't) or rescued someone from their own responsibilities.

It can seem so much easier to try to avoid feeling bad by smoothing things over, and keeping the peace. We all do this sometimes, because we want to be accepted and validated by others. We also do it because we want to avoid conflict.

I know that even just the thought of challenging someone's disrespect can seem daunting—ruffling their feathers means you may well have to sit with the discomfort for a while. But this is life. There will always be differences of opinions and flurries of emotions. If we can learn to be more honest about our need for regard and respect (even in small steps), life can move forward instead of stagnating, because those same old issues won't keep popping up time and again.

And respect works both ways. When we're not being honest with someone about how we feel—is that being respectful to ourselves? Is it being respectful to them?

I want to be clear here that I'm not suggesting being honest to the point of blatant *un*kindness. I wouldn't be so tactless as to tell someone they look awful today, purely in the interests of being authentic! What I'm talking about here is when we consistently try to avoid upsetting the apple cart so we can have a quiet life—and all the while ignoring that inner voice that tells us we deserve better.

When Sam finally, lovingly, took the courage to be authentic and tell Fay it was time to get her act together, he was no longer enabling her self-destructive and disrespectful behaviour. Fay complained a bit, she sulked for a couple of days, and then she did get her act together. She was able to move forward in her life, and their relationship grew stronger because ultimately she realised that Sam truly cared.

Like everyone else, it's likely that you can identify times in your life where you've used misguided kindness. Possibly quite often. Don't judge yourself for this though—everyone does it. It's just a muddled-up way of viewing 'being kind'. That's why I call it *misguided* kindness, because I want you to understand that it's not that you're doing anything wrong—it's just that it's so very easy to get confused.

Conscious Kindness

While misguided kindness is often a knee-jerk reaction—an attempt to smooth things over and keep people happy—conscious kindness is the opposite. As the word 'conscious' implies, it's much more about self-reflection and thinking things through. It's about considering the long-term outcome and it's about finding the balance of positive outcome and love for all concerned. You'll see as we look more at conscious kindness that this is at the heart of assertiveness.

Conscious kindness asks:

- How can I respect myself, and others, by being authentic in this situation?
- How can I make sure I'm being kind to both myself *and* the other person here?
- What does our relationship need from me for it to evolve and deepen?

It takes a little practice to think in this more intentional way, but you'll find that once you make this shift, it's so much easier to be sincere and direct in your relationships. The more you practise conscious kindness, the easier it will be to find the courage to be your authentic self and speak your truth.

Sam had been putting off confronting the situation with Fay because he feared rejection. It's this fear that, even when it may not be at the surface of awareness, is behind misguided kindness.

When Sam realised that his reluctance to confront Fay wasn't helping, he found the courage to overcome his fear and challenge her behaviour. By looking at the broader picture and wanting to truly help her and their relationship, he made the shift to approach the problem from a place of love—instead of fear and worry.

I often talk about the power of love, because I've seen, through helping so many people, that when we make the decision to come from a place of love, we're given the strength and guidance we need.

One Small Step at a Time

This isn't to say that a magic wand is waved, and a person will suddenly become all brightness and light. Sam had to sit with discomfort for a day or two while Fay sulked and then figured things out. Learning to be more assertive is a process: it takes practice, one small step at a time.

There's no rule that says you must suddenly change into a

SELF-ASSURED SUPERHERO overnight! It's more a step-by-step journey towards the confident you.

A self-assured life is a cumulative process:

The more you say no, the easier it becomes to say no.

The less you people-please, the less you'll need to people-please.

The more you speak up, the easier it will become to speak up.

The more you ask for respect, the easier it will become to ask for respect.

Navigating relationships can be challenging, but so very rewarding when we get it right. As you begin to practise a more conscious kindness, you'll see that people come around surprisingly quickly. Especially when they detect that you're coming from a place of love.

You can also tell people that you're practising being more confident and assertive. This way they won't be taken aback by your new way of being. Often, they'll be inspired to join you on your quest for a more intentional life!

Your Conscious Kindness Checklist

Learning to be consciously kind can take a little work, especially if you've been in the habit of smoothing things over. With that in mind, I've provided a **Conscious Kindness Checklist** to help guide you. You can get the downloadable PDF version of this checklist with your free companion course at the website. I strongly encourage you to print it out. It's a handy checklist of questions which will help you find clarity in confusing situations.

www.howkindpeople.com

Here's a brief sum up:

MISGUIDED KINDNESS	CONSCIOUS KINDNESS
Is hidden behind a mask	Is authentic
Is out of balance: favours one person over another	Is in balance: sees the bigger picture which includes everyone
Feels shaky or chaotic	Has boundaries and feels grounded
Brings up feelings of guilt, frustration, resentment, fear, or confusion	Brings up feelings of satisfaction, security, love, and clarity
Takes away confidence	Increases confidence
Is a short-term fix	Takes a little time and courage and then reaps long-term benefits
Is not assertive	Is assertive

Knowing Where You're Starting From

Practical tools and techniques, such as communication skills, boundary setting, and confidence techniques are an essential part of becoming more assertive, and you'll find plenty of these within the pages of this book. However, before I share them, I want to make sure that you'll find them effective.

As we've seen, learning to be assertive isn't just about finding the right tools and techniques—before you apply them, you need to have an understanding of what these changes will mean for your life.

Any change is like a journey. It's a process with a beginning and an end. It's the same with learning to be more confident and assertive. It's important to acknowledge the beginning: *this is where I am at*, in order to be able to take the steps to the end: *this is where I want to be.*

The problem I've found is that people often struggle with the beginning part—with fully accepting themselves for where they are currently at in life. They're so caught up in self-criticism and self-judgement about their mistakes and their lack of assertiveness, they can't lovingly accept themselves so they keep themselves stuck in resistance. It's like trying to get from A to B, but not accepting that you're at A to start with.

I see this sometimes when a new client tells me that they

feel embarrassed—ashamed even—for 'having to come to therapy'. And each time I hear this, it still manages to surprise me, because I know that coming to therapy is one of the most courageous and responsible things a person can do.

There's nothing shameful about having therapy: it's to be applauded! Coming to therapy is like opening your eyes and saying, 'This is where I'm at. This is my A. I'm human, I have my vulnerabilities, and that's OK. Now that I'm accepting where I'm starting from, I can move forward. So show me how to get to B!'

It's the same with learning to be more assertive. The fact is that most of us are *not* good at being assertive at all. It isn't a natural skill for human beings. So it's hugely important to stop blaming and criticising ourselves for our vulnerabilities and accept that assertiveness is challenging for everyone. Once we do this, then we have a great starting point for moving forward.

I want to spend a little time now looking at the fundamental reasons why assertiveness can be such a challenge for people so that you can get a very clear picture of why you may have been struggling too.

Once you get clear on this, you'll let go of any inner resistance, and you'll find it easy to move forward into the new, more self-assured version of yourself.

Part Two

Why Do We Find It So Hard to be Assertive?

The chances are that you already know what you need to say, or do, in order to feel more confident and improve your relationship: maybe with one person in your life, or maybe in a few relationships.

Perhaps you've already read books or taken courses to help with building confidence and becoming more self-assured. Maybe you've discovered some great tools and techniques, but when you've come to apply them, you've struggled and given up because it's been too challenging.

So you've continued to let it go when you've been disrespected, or you've carried on being kind in misguided ways, because even though that inner voice keeps telling you that you deserve better, stepping out from behind your mask and asking for better treatment just doesn't seem to work for you.

How and Why You May be Sabotaging Yourself

As any good therapist will tell you, it's very hard for a client to make changes if they're continually beating themselves up for having the problem in the first place. Seeing lack of assertiveness as a problem in yourself that *must be fixed* simply creates resistance—it's pushing against the problem, rather than allowing the process of change to happen.

For example, when we keep thinking

'Why am I like this?'

'What's wrong with me?'

'I should have stood up for myself!'

'Why can't I change?'

we create resistance. That's not giving any leeway for change to take place.

As I often say to my clients, 'You wouldn't speak to a small child in this way and then expect them to feel confident. So why would you speak to yourself like this and expect positive results?'

Once you begin to think thoughts, such as

'Everyone feels like this sometimes.'

'It's a normal human condition.'

'I'm working on it.'

you'll stop knocking your own confidence. You'll be coming from a place of self-love, instead of staying stuck, immobilised in fear.

Certainly, love is always the antidote for fear, and fear is always behind our challenges with asserting ourselves. Fear makes itself known through fundamental human struggles, creating blocks so that we find it hard to step into the light and speak our truth.

Once we identify these blocks, we can tackle them, and move past them. These blocks are:

- Fear of Rejection from the Tribe
- Limiting Beliefs
- Misplaced Empathy
- When Emotions Hold Us Hostage

Let's explore how each of these impacts our ability to be assertive. Then we'll go on to look at how to get past these blocks.

Chapter 4
Rejection from the Tribe

Can you remember a time when you felt rejected? It's a horrible feeling, isn't it? It can feel like an actual physical pain—as though someone has reached in and tugged out your heart.

Our first experiences of rejection happen in childhood. They can feel very intense. A lot of people can recall experiences like these:

- Feeling rejected by a parent who didn't pay attention to them
- Being shunned by other children in the playground
- Being teased by older siblings
- Feeling hurt because a teacher didn't notice them.

As time passes, whether or not we have clear memories of these intensely painful experiences, they do remain in the subconscious. In adult life, when we have another experience of being rejected, we re-experience those same powerful emotions. Psychologists will often describe this as 'going into child' because it's the little child within us who is remembering and feeling these distressing experiences.

We could say that all children are vulnerable to rejection—even those who have the safest and most secure of upbringings—purely because they are so dependent on their caregivers. As a child you were small, and the caregivers in your life, such as parents and teachers, were big. They weren't just big in stature—they were also *big* in terms of power. It's only natural that you would have craved their attention and approval because you needed them to take care of you. You needed them to give you food and shelter and to keep you safe from harm. The worst thing that could have happened would have been to be rejected by them. Deep down it was all about survival.

The Tribe

Now let's take this concept a little further. Children need adults to take care of them, and adults need each other. We are social animals. Our ancestors survived by living in groups. Tribes.

This is why asserting ourselves can feel so risky. Inherently, we feel driven to maintain relationships with each other in order to keep ourselves safe. We do this by:

- Trying to be liked, approved of and accepted: we want to draw people towards us.

- Avoiding conflict and hostility: we don't want to push people away.

The reality is that when we step forward and speak our truth, someone may well be upset, at least for a while. At best the issue will be resolved, at worst it may mean the end of a relationship, but ultimately, we will survive.

However, on a primal level, we carry this innate fear that if we assert ourselves, we'll be rejected and will be cast out of the tribe. No food, no shelter. We will not survive. We will die!

Return now to the twenty-first century and it seems illogical that we could run our lives based on such a primal fear—but we all do. So the next time you find yourself fearing rejection if you assert yourself, take courage. After all, if you say no to a friend, does that really mean you'll be banned by society for the rest of your life?

Even the most confident of people can find it hard to assert themselves some of the time. The trick is to recognise that this fear is a natural part of human life, and stop trying to avoid it.

Ravi, 24

Ravi moved to a new town and quickly made friends. Every Saturday night, they would all go to a bar. Ravi would always volunteer to be the designated driver because he wanted to be kind, and he felt good that the others all liked him for it. However, he was getting fed up because driving meant he couldn't have a drink, relax, and not have to worry about looking after everyone.

Ravi decided to tell them that he didn't want to be the designated driver every time, but he worried that they wouldn't invite him out again.

The following Saturday morning, he received a text:

> We're out tonight, mate! Is your car out of the garage yet?

Ravi was greatly tempted to pretend his car was still in the garage so he could wriggle out of having to speak up. He knew in his heart though, that it was time to be his true self. It was a risk. He'd be making himself vulnerable to rejection. However, he also knew that he needed to be kind to himself—a conscious kindness.

He took courage, and replied:

> Car's passed its fitness test, thanks. I'm not driving tonight though —who is?

Ravi worried when he didn't get an immediate reply. Then an hour later his phone beeped.

> I've been in touch with Kate and she'll do it. She'll pick you up at 7pm.

Ravi realised he'd been worrying about nothing. It was simply that his friends had become used to him doing the driving.

Ravi's worries about being excluded from the group is a classic example of the human struggle with being more assertive. Something doesn't feel right; we want to speak up but fear of rejection stops us in our tracks.

By taking the courage to be more assertive, Ravi was able to forge a closer connection with his new friends because he now knew for sure that they liked him for himself, rather than just for his chauffeuring services. Had they simply been using him for a lift, would they really have been such good friends? It's only when we test the waters that we find out if this is the 'tribe' we really want to be a part of.

This deeply innate fear of being cast out of the tribe is common to all human beings. It's one very big reason that we struggle to step into the light and be our authentic selves. And, as life goes on, we may have experiences of rejection which only reinforce this fear—yet we do well to remember that while rejection can be a painful experience, it sorts out the wheat from the chaff. It makes space to forge stronger, more healthy and meaningful relationships.

Chapter 5
Limiting Beliefs

Most people have some beliefs that are unhelpful, impacting their confidence negatively. These beliefs are often called limiting beliefs. Here are some that come up in the therapy room, particularly around the subject of being more assertive. Perhaps they'll be familiar to you.

- If I say no, it makes me look mean.
- I'm not good enough unless other people say so.
- I mustn't put myself first, because that's selfish.
- I must be liked by everyone.
- I can avoid upsets by keeping people happy.
- If I please people, they'll never let me down.

I've met many clients who've easily recognised the limiting beliefs that have been affecting their confidence. However they're extremely frustrated, because even though they see these so clearly, they still can't seem to change. They say things like 'I have a terrible habit of people-pleasing. I don't know why I can't seem to stop it!' or 'I do understand that it's OK to say no in theory, but when I open my mouth, yes comes out!'

So, what exactly are limiting beliefs? Where do they come from, and why do they have such a firm hold over us?

If You Feel It, It Must Matter

Here's how a belief is formed. You have an experience which causes you to feel a strong emotion. Therefore, that experience matters to you. And because the experience has caused strong emotion, and thus matters, you then draw some conclusion about it. It is this conclusion that is the basis of your belief.

Experience + Emotional Response + Conclusion = BELIEF

This is true for us at all stages of life, and it's especially striking in childhood. Have you noticed how small children can experience emotions so intensely? They can be in floods of tears one minute, and fits of giggles the next!

Because of this emotional intensity, some experiences, such as being ignored or teased can have long-lasting effects, because a child will draw a conclusion about what that must mean about themselves. Their conclusion is the start of a limiting belief. It could be something like 'I'm not good enough,' or 'I'm not worthy of being loved'.

Another reason beliefs take such a firm hold is explained by neuroscience, and again it's much to do with childhood. Between the ages of around two and seven years old, children need to be able to take in a vast amount of information in order to help them grow and develop—there's a lot happening between toddlerhood and primary school. Their brainwaves, vibrating at a specific frequency called theta, help them absorb this information. And while this helps them grow, it also means they tend to just accept that everything is true.

Your Modus Operandi

Children continually refine and tweak their beliefs according to the reactions they get from others. Without even being aware of it, they decide 'If I do this, then that happens, so I need to do this to make people like me, and that way I'll be safe, sheltered, and loved.'

As children, then, we all form a personal system of beliefs, and it becomes a kind of modus operandi for life: a programme which runs automatically in the subconscious, like information on a hard drive, and dictates how we think, feel, and behave.

Given that scientific research now tells us that the subconscious mind dictates around 95% of our thoughts and decisions, we can see that this doesn't leave much room for the conscious mind to make new choices and maintain them.

This is why people can often see the changes they need to make, but then struggle to make those changes. The conscious part of their mind is saying something like 'Hey, I'm going to be more assertive. I'm going to say no next time.' But the subconscious mind jumps in, saying, 'Hang on, I've got a belief about that—it's dangerous. Be careful! You don't want to be seen as unkind, and you especially don't want to risk being rejected!'

What's important, though, is that you remember that your own unhelpful beliefs are not *bad* beliefs—they are *limiting* beliefs. And why the word 'limiting'? Because they are not suitable for your stage of life now.

When you were a child, those beliefs made perfect sense, because they kept you happy and secure. Children's relationships are straightforward. If, as a child, saying yes and being good meant you got love and attention in return, well of course it would make sense to say yes. If you said no, and got reprimanded for being naughty and argumentative, well of course it was a bad idea to say no. So, believing that Yes was better than No was a good belief—back then.

The problem is that because the subconscious is so powerful, we tend to continue operating from these outmoded belief systems. If we are to form more adult relationships, based on mutual respect and regard, we need to let these beliefs go. We need to find new healthier beliefs. This is perfectly possible to achieve with some awareness, and the correct tools and techniques.

Alex, 7 and 27

When Alex was seven years old, life was difficult at home. His parents were splitting up. There was often a lot of conflict; his parents would shout at each other, and quite often they'd tell him off for being naughty, when he didn't think he had been.

Alex had always been good at maths, and now he discovered that absorbing himself in maths problems took his mind off his worries. Alex's teacher was so impressed by his hard work. He constantly praised Alex for all the extra work he put into his maths and gave him lots of attention and validation. Alex beamed with pleasure and happiness at every compliment from his teacher. All this helped young Alex get through one of the most difficult times in his life. He formed the belief that working extra hard meant validation, getting attention, and security.

Twenty years later, Alex was working in a busy surveyor's office. He had a fair bit of responsibility and took the job seriously. He didn't think twice about taking extra work home, and he was always eager to please his boss. However, the more work Alex took on, the more his boss expected of him. Plus, his colleagues took advantage of him. They would often wriggle their way out of jobs, leaving him to take the load. Added to that, he'd just been passed up for a promotion by someone who only seemed to do half as much work as he did!

The problem was that the very belief that had once helped Alex ('If I work extra hard, I'll get attention and approval.') had turned out to work against him in his adult life.

Adult relationships are so much more complex than those of childhood. Adults communicate in subtle ways—we give each other messages about how we expect to be treated. We do this by how we behave and how we treat ourselves. Working very hard was a form of people-pleasing that had been a fantastic idea when Alex was seven years old. It got him the validation he craved. Now, however, it was resulting in people simply taking him for granted.

The Subconscious Doesn't Differentiate Time

Whether or not we have clear memories of distressing experiences from childhood, they are always there in the subconscious. Then, in adult life, when we have another similar experience, we replay those same intense emotions. We feel the same fears, because the subconscious doesn't differentiate time—it doesn't know that many years have passed since the experience happened. In an instant, we emotionally time-travel back to the small vulnerable child we once were, and so we often react just as we did then.

During our sessions, Alex was able to see more clearly

that his need to please had originated from his childhood experiences. It gave him permission to consider life from a different, more adult perspective.

Much as this was significant progress, Alex was still beating himself up for his previous lack of assertiveness. I pointed out that there was nothing to be gained by judging himself.

It's never helpful to look back with regret, wishing we'd been different in the past—it's a waste of time and energy. If you can identify that you've been operating your life from unhelpful beliefs, don't sabotage your progress now by dwelling on that—doing so will only create resistance and keep you stuck.

Remember that a confident life is a work in progress, and self-acceptance is a big part of that journey. I have found, though, that people often get confused about that. They think that accepting themselves as they are means letting themselves off the hook. They're so hard on themselves. The secret is that once you accept that you have a limiting belief and that it's OK—you are human—you'll let go of the resistance to it. This means you give yourself calm and space to put techniques to work that can help you let that limiting belief go. Then you can replace it with a more helpful belief, such as 'I'm good enough just as I am'.

To find out more about techniques to let go of limiting beliefs, I suggest you also read *Out Of Fear Into Love: Life doesn't have to be a struggle.*

Quick Win

One handy tip to help identify limiting beliefs is to notice when you're using exaggerated language. Words such as *always, never, no one, should, must, everyone*, and *won't* are indicators.

Here's an example. 'I can never say what I really want, because if I do, no one will like me.' When you notice yourself using these types of exaggerated words, don't get annoyed and try to force them away—that will just cause resistance. Accept that you've used them, and then follow them up with more realistic words, such as *sometimes, occasionally, some people, possibly, may not*, or *could*.

Here's the example from above, rephrased: 'I *sometimes* find it hard to say what I want, because I think that if do, some people *may not* like me.'

And given that *sometimes* is not *never*, you can even take this a step further with: 'There are times when *it's easier* to say what I want, and *maybe some* people *don't actually* mind.'

I suggest you make a practice of writing down your revised

statements. Writing them down is in itself a powerful tool for priming your subconscious to begin thinking differently.

So far, we've seen that an innate fear of rejection from the tribe and our learnt beliefs make it difficult for many of us to be assertive. Now, let's explore the other two reasons we struggle: misplaced empathy and overwhelming emotions.

Chapter 6
Misplaced Empathy

The founder of Analytical Psychology, Carl Jung, is famous for having said, 'All therapists are wounded healers.' By that, he meant that because they've had their own personal struggles and challenges, therapists are more easily able to identify with their clients. This is true. Many therapists are naturally empathic because their own challenging experiences have led them to an interest in the human condition. They've navigated their way to their own healing, and consequently have a desire to help others do the same.

However, therapists are taught to use their natural tendency for empathy in a very specific way. They're trained to step into their clients' shoes: they're right there with them on a deeply knowing and connected level, whilst keeping the focus completely away from themselves.

And much as they care deeply, therapists are *consciously* kind in the way they help their clients. That is, they hold strong boundaries so that they're able to keep themselves and their clients safe while still offering them empathy. It's a learnt skill.

This is where a lot of people run into trouble. Not being trained therapists, they've never had the opportunity to learn these skills, and so the boundaries get blurred. No wonder it's hard to be assertive when challenges arise. In their attempts to be kind and compassionate, they give out all the wrong messages, allowing others to cross the line.

Imagine a therapist who had great empathy for their client, because they too had once had a similar problem. Now, imagine that this therapist, knowing how bad that client must feeling, told them that they'd be available for them any time, night or day. Also, that the client didn't need to pay them, because they know what it's like to be short of money. We can see how absurd this is, and detrimental. The client needs to have some sense of boundaries, to feel contained and strong in themselves, rather than weak and reliant on the therapist.

The use of appropriate boundaries, then, is clear in the therapist's room, but it's a very different story in everyday life. Lack of appropriate boundaries is very common, and even when people get good at setting them, they can slip back into old patterns because they worry about being unkind. So they get carried away with empathy. Then, realising that perhaps they've been a little too tolerant and giving, they have to rethink the situation.

Setting and maintaining boundaries, then, is a powerful—and essential—tool for leading an assertive life. We're going to be revisiting boundaries a lot as we go through the chapters because they are so very important. I'll be showing you some easy ways to set them—and maintain them.

But I Don't Want to be the Baddie!

Another reason we can misplace empathy is through fear of how we'll be judged. Every one of us goes through difficult times in life. They may be traumas in childhood, they may be situations that arise in later years. We all have losses and struggles, hurts and rejections. So, we all know what it feels like to be in emotional pain.

And since we are kind and caring, we naturally empathise with others because we don't want them to feel that same distress. We certainly don't want to feel like we're the cause of it!

As I mentioned in chapter 1 'Who Are The Kind People?' human beings have a tendency to categorise each other, assigning people roles of goodie or baddie. This often means that if we want to confront someone about their poor behaviour, we can have the mistaken notion that doing so will make *us* the bad ones.

We think 'If I get cross because you're treating me so badly, then I am treating you badly ... I don't want to hurt your feelings ... I don't want to be seen as the bad one.'

To be more assertive though, as I've mentioned, sometimes we need to be kind enough to be willing to sit with our own discomfort for a while. That's the conscious type of kindness, which ultimately gives the other person the opportunity to process the situation—and maybe even learn something that will help them in the long run.

For some people, though, misplacing empathy isn't just an occasional thing—it's a learnt habit which causes ongoing problems for their relationships, and continuously knocks their confidence. This habit often starts in childhood. For example, those children who have to take on too much responsibility have to grow up before their time. Consequently, they'll go on to become adults who don't always notice that other people have responsibility for themselves.

It's like a blind spot—an unhelpful and limiting set of beliefs which drives how they think and feel about having to take responsibility.

The belief system goes something along the lines of:

It's probably my fault.

If they do something to upset me and I let them know, then I'm at fault for causing them distress.

I don't want to be the cause of their pain.

Mike, 32

When Mike was just eleven years old, his mother walked out and left the family. It was a terrible time for him. His father started drinking heavily and stopped taking care of the house, and he and his younger sister were left to their own devices.

Mike adopted the role of grown-up, taking care of the house and his sister. He lost touch with his friends because he never had time to play. He missed his mother desperately. During our sessions he recalled the sheer and utter loneliness he had felt. A young boy all alone in an adult world.

Mike grew up. He met Nadia, who had a three-year-old son Nicky, who adored Mike. It wasn't a good relationship with Nadia though. She didn't treat Mike very well; she had cheated on him twice; she was disrespectful, often putting him down in front of her friends. Mike would try to laugh it off, but inside he was in great emotional pain.

Mike knew he wasn't being authentic. His heart told him that he should walk away, but he couldn't bear to abandon little Nicky, or even Nadia. After all, he knew what it was like to have someone walk out of your life.

Such was Mike's need to avoid hurting them that he was thinking only in terms of 'Should I stay or should I leave?' It's common to think like this when we're under stress. The brain goes into Yes/No mode—a survival response to stress. If you've ever found yourself trying to make a difficult decision in the face of someone treating you badly, you may recall a similar type of all-or-nothing thinking. It keeps you stuck because your thoughts go around and around, and you just keep swinging back and forth in your decision.

In our sessions, Mike came to see that there might be some middle ground. Instead of dealing with Nadia's disrespect by painfully bearing it, or leaving, he could try being more intentional about his relationship and set some healthy boundaries. If Nadia was unwilling or unable to respect those, it would be her own responsibility if she lost the relationship with him—not his.

I've met many people like Mike, who have had this mistaken belief system around empathy. I was the same, until I learnt that it's actually a much kinder act to allow people to take responsibility for themselves—it means they get to grow.

We Are Responsible *To*, Not *For*

If you find yourself stuck in a situation where you're not sure of the boundaries around empathy, a useful way to approach it is to remember the following: we are responsible *to*. We are not responsible *for*.

As kind people, we all have a responsibility to offer each other respect, consideration, and compassion. However, we're *not* responsible *for* another adult person. Only they can take responsibility for the choices they make, and the consequences of those choices. Getting a grasp on this difference between *to* and *for* is a powerful way to let go of the misplaced empathy habit. It will give you courage.

This brings me to the last point about why we find it so hard to be assertive, and that is when emotions hold us hostage. Let's look at this now. Then we'll go on to start applying practical ways for you to step into the new, more self-assured, version of you.

Chapter 7
When Emotions Hold Us Hostage

Gareth, 47

Gareth and his son Ben had fallen out. Gareth hadn't been around much when Ben was growing up, and for Ben, now twenty-two, there was a lot of hurt and pain from his childhood that had never been resolved. It had all culminated in a huge row three months earlier.

Emotions had run high, and now even though a few months had passed by, Gareth was still feeling very anxious about it. At the time, Ben, in a state of fury, had told his father that he never wanted to speak to him again. Gareth was at a loss as to what to do—would they ever be able to talk again? Every time Gareth thought about trying to contact Ben, he would feel panicky.

Ben's birthday was coming up and he very much wanted to send him a card, but he was full of anxiety about what reaction he might get. 'I keep going around in circles,' he said.

'One of the things he brought up was that I always forgot his birthday when he was growing up. I want to send a card now, but I'm not sure if he'll take it the wrong way.'

To send a card would make Gareth vulnerable because it could invite even more anger from Ben. On the other hand, he didn't want to *not* send a card. He couldn't decide what to do.

Gareth was making a mistake that many of us make in these types of situations. Rather than simply asking a person how they feel, we try to second guess them because we're trying to limit any potential upset. It's far more effective to be transparent though.

'Have you asked him how he'd take it if you sent a card?' I hinted. Gareth sent the following email to Ben:

> I know we're not speaking, and we have things to figure out. But your birthday is coming up and I'd really like to send you a card.
>
> I don't want to upset you. I'm worried that if I just send it, you may send it back, or rip it up, and that would hurt us both.
>
> So, I thought I'd ask first. If I send you a card will you accept it in the goodwill it is meant? A temporary truce at least?

Ben replied that he'd be pleased to get the card. It was a turning point. They still had their issues to work through, but by taking the courage to make himself vulnerable, Gareth had made a good step in the right direction—for them both.

It's difficult to be courageous when emotions overwhelm us. Maybe you can relate to Gareth. Perhaps there's been a time in your life where you had some challenging situation which led to your emotions taking control? Or it's experiences from childhood that cause overwhelming emotions to reappear in your current relationships.

Perhaps a challenging situation arises with someone, and you don't agree with their point of view, or you feel disrespected in some way. You want to say something, to speak up and assert yourself, but you just can't! You notice your heart is pounding, your stomach is churning—maybe your palms are sweaty. If you do manage to say something, your words come out all garbled and your voice sounds high-pitched and squeaky.

These types of physical reactions are common to all of us. It's to do with a part of the brain called the amygdala.

Your Amygdala is Trying to Protect You

You've maybe heard of the Fight or Flight Response. When we feel threatened in a situation (physically or emotionally), we either go into Fight Mode, getting angry and defensive, or we go into Flight Mode, withdrawing from the situation as soon as possible.

What's less commonly known is Freeze Mode. When we go into Freeze Mode, we shut down. Have you ever been so stressed that you can't remember the simplest of things? That's Freeze Mode. It's the same when you want to speak up and assert yourself, but your mind goes blank. It's a perfectly natural neurobiological event, and it's the amygdala that's causing it.

When we have an experience that we - often subconsciously - perceive to be threatening in some way, the amygdala goes into action to help protect us. It does this by making us feel strong emotions, such as anger, fear, or confusion urging us to fight, run away, or freeze.

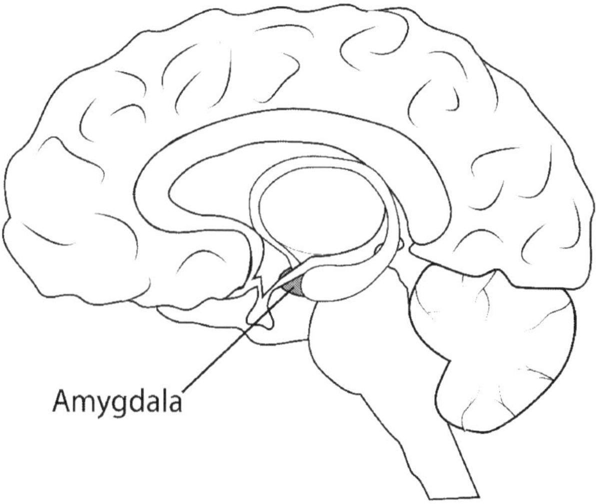

It's great that this part of the brain wants to protect us, but it often acts in inappropriate ways for modern-day living.

Many thousands of years ago, when we lived in untamed environments where dangerous animals posed a threat to our survival, it was a good idea that emotions took over because it meant that we had a better chance of staying alive.

But today, the things that trigger our stress are completely different. It's more about trying to manage complex relationships than sabre-toothed tigers chasing us down the high street! The problem is that the amygdala doesn't know that this is the twenty-first century—and so it continues on, valiantly trying to protect us from this 'danger' by overwhelming our emotions and triggering our actions. It's no wonder we find it so hard to be firm and speak our truth when emotions are overwhelming us. What's needed is to get good at mastering those emotions.

Fear, Guilt, and Resentment

In helping people learn to be more confident and speak up, I've seen that there are three common emotions which often cause problems for them. They are fear, guilt, and resentment.

Fear happens because we worry that in asserting ourselves, we'll either invite conflict, or we'll be rejected. Neither one is a good outcome. It's fear that drives misguided kindness: we want to smooth things over and not have to worry.

Guilt can often happen when we're considering being more assertive. It's often about misplaced empathy: we don't want to hurt someone's feelings; we don't want to be the baddie in the situation, so we hold back. I believe that on some deeply psychological level, we use guilt as a way of signalling to ourselves that we must be one of the good, kind, and caring people. After all we wouldn't feel *so bad* if we didn't care!

Resentment tends to come when we've already allowed a situation to happen. Maybe we've ignored someone's disrespect, or not spoken up and said no. Later we are exasperated with ourselves, wishing we'd spoken up and possibly even blaming the other person for having 'made us' agree to something.

It's useful to recognise that these emotions of fear, guilt, and resentment can never go hand in hand with assertiveness. To be confident and true to ourselves, we must operate from a place of adult, consciously considered responses. Given that human beings are often naturally emotional creatures, that can make it difficult. So we need to find ways to manage these emotions, rather than allowing them to creep up and hold us hostage.

Your Feelings are *Your* Feelings

Do remember though, that how you feel is always valid. If someone tells you that you shouldn't be feeling the way you do, please don't take that on board. Your feelings are *your* feelings—they are always valid for you. However, it may well be it's the way you are reacting to the situation that is a little askew, and that's probably what the person is really referring to.

It's also important to remember that while none of us like to experience negative and overwhelming emotions, those emotions are there to help us. They are the signals of what is really going on. Sometimes we ignore things, but our emotions never lie—they'll always tell us if we're allowing others to mistreat us, or not treating ourselves very well. So it's extremely important that we get good at listening to the messages our emotions send us.

But it's not just about listening to the messages, it's also about dealing with the emotions themselves. Think of it like this. If a messenger came to you and said, 'Look, I just want to let you know that there's an issue here. You need to work out this problem.'

Well, that would be a good thing. However, what if that messenger wouldn't leave your side, and they kept pestering you and shouting, 'Sort out your problem! Sort out your problem!' That wouldn't be so helpful! You wouldn't be able to focus on finding a solution with all that racket going on! So, even though your emotions are wonderful messengers to alert you when change needs to happen, and it's important that you acknowledge them, it's also important to check if they are overwhelming you. If they are, you need to find ways to send them on their way.

It's Little Wonder that So Many of Us Struggle

So, it is little wonder that so many of us struggle to step into the light and be our authentic selves. Primal fears of being cast out of the tribe, individual experiences in childhood, unhelpful beliefs lodged in the subconscious, misplaced empathy and overwhelming emotions—all these make it hard for us to assert ourselves. As we continue on through the chapters, I'll be referring to these, and I'll be sharing ways to overcome them in specific situations and scenarios.

You've already taken several steps towards the confident you. Together, we've been building a foundation of understanding, self-acceptance, and awareness. We've looked at what kindness means, and how when we consider the right *kind* of kind—conscious kindness—we can be caring, considerate, and assertive all at the same time.

Preparing

Part Three

An Intentional Life

Chapter 8
Your Intentional Life Plan

Some people think that life just happens in a random fashion. They wish for things to turn out a certain way, then sit back and cross their fingers.

I can tell by the fact that you're reading this book that you're *not* one of those people. You understand that those of us who lead a happy, confident, and successful life do so because we are intentional about it.

Ultimately, there is no person or situation in charge of our lives—except ourselves. That's why leading a more confident life begins with being intentional about how we think and what we do; it's about stepping into the light and taking full responsibility for our own happiness.

Getting Clear: is it Me or is it Them?

Making the decision to be more assertive in your life is one thing, but putting that into practice is not always so straightforward. You may find yourself feeling confused and wondering: 'Am I right to be pressing my point here, or am I just being oversensitive? ... Is this really my stuff, or is it their stuff?... Is it my place to say something?... Is there something else going on here that isn't so obvious to me?'

You may decide to talk over your concerns with a good friend or a family member who can offer you guidance, and this can be very helpful if that person has wisdom and has been living their own assertive life. Sometimes, though, we can seek advice from friends and family, only to end up feeling more confused than ever. This is because the advisor is giving an opinion based on their own personal life experiences.

The solution is for you yourself to become very clear on your own guidelines. It's about deciding

- How you want to be treated by others
- How you want to treat yourself
- How you want to treat others.

One very good way to get this clarity is to create a written piece of content where you declare what you want for your life, and most importantly, where you provide yourself with some clear structure and guidelines on how you're going to achieve that.

By creating this written piece of content, you're taking wishes and ideas from your mind and making them manifest in reality. You now have clarity, plus a personal guide to refer to. This in itself means you'll have already started to become the new, more assertive version of you.

Do remember also that your guidelines are yours. No one can tell you what values you should hold or what boundaries to have in your relationships.

In the following chapters, I'm going to be walking you through some simple steps which will help you create your personal guide. I have called this guide your **Intentional Life Plan**. It will give you a reference point so that when you're in different future situations that require you to be more assertive, you can refer back to it. It's like having a personal mentor!

Your **Intentional Life Plan** consists of three sections.

- Section One: Identifying Your Rewards
- Section Two: Creating Your Vision
- Section Three: Choosing Your Guidelines

Tips on Filling in Your **Intentional Life Plan**

To make creating your plan an easy process, I have provided templates for you at the website.

You can either:

Download, print and fill them in on paper

Or

Fill in the fillable PDF version at the website and save to your device.

www.howkindpeople.com

Sections One and Two of your plan can be filled in at any point from now. Section Three refers to the upcoming chapters. You may like to stop and fill in the first two sections now, or you may like to read through the whole book, and come back to your plan later. Either way, I can't say strongly enough how helpful it will be for you to complete the **Intentional Life Plan**. It will bring you great benefits, as it has done for so many of my clients.

Section One: Identifying Your Rewards

In Section One you'll be identifying how being more assertive will reward and enrich your life, and your relationships. This is an important first step because we humans have a tendency to resist change. No matter how much we want it on the one hand, we resist it on the other. So, to deal with that resistance, we need some sort of payoff—a way to see that life will be better once we nudge ourselves out of our comfort zone. This section of the plan then, will get you started by helping you focus on how much your life will improve: you'll have a good incentive to make changes.

You can find your template PDF to complete this section of

your **Intentional Life Plan** at www.howkindpeople.com

Section Two: Creating Your Vision

On any journey, in order to reach your destination, you must know where you're headed. Imagine being on a journey and when people ask, 'Where are you going?' you say, 'I don't really know, I'm just trying to get away from the last place!' Yet we very often take this approach to life's problems, and then wonder why we keep going around in circles.

In Section Two, then, you'll be creating your vision—you'll be considering what your new assertive life will look like. Who will you become? I can't say strongly enough here that creating your vision is paramount in changing your life.

While this section of your plan is all about vision, don't worry if you're not a particularly visual person. You'll see in the templates that I walk you through it step by step.

We have seen the power of the subconscious in directing our thoughts, feelings, and behaviours. However, rather than being a slave to its programming, we can utilise that power to achieve what we want. Having a vision also means, then, priming your subconscious. The subconscious *must* follow the directions it is given. Once you create a specific and clear vision of the new assertive you, your subconscious will begin seeking out signposts and opportunities to help you get there.

You can experiment with this vision, imagining yourself in different roles and scenarios, speaking up, saying no, setting boundaries, and asking for respect.

As you begin to envision yourself in this new version, you may well find that emotions come up—you may even feel a little anxious.

Don't worry if this happens: it's normal. Just let yourself know that it's only a game in your head—you don't have to do anything for now—just play around with the idea of how things *could* be different.

You can find your template PDF to complete this section of your **Intentional Life Plan** at www.howkindpeople.com

Section Three: Choosing Your Guidelines

Once you have considered the rewards and come up with a vision of the new you, it's time to decide on a specific set of personal guidelines to make being assertive an easy and natural process.

We each have our own values and ideas about how we want to behave, and how we want to be treated. It's a personal thing, and it can be hard to get clear on this. So, this section of the **Intentional Life Plan** is geared towards helping you clarify your guidelines and boundaries.

You'll find a handy worksheet on boundaries, followed by templates with questions specific to each chapter topic. They'll help you plan ahead for how you want to be in different scenarios and situations in your life. You'll notice that at the end of each upcoming chapter, I've provided a few self-reflective questions to help you start mulling over some ideas for choosing these guidelines and boundaries.

Taking Action

I recently came across a quote which deeply touched my heart. It's from the book *Little Women* by Louisa May Alcott. It is:

'I am not afraid of storms, for I am learning to sail my ship.'

It made me think about my clients, my own life, and all of us. About how we sometimes struggle because we're trying to deal with problems without any help. If we have no guidance, no tools or strategies, then those problems can seem like battling through a raging sea.

Yet when we have the right tools and strategies, we can ride out the storm, we can navigate through unknown waters, and we can steer our way to calmer seas. We can learn to sail our ship.

Many of us were never taught assertiveness and communication skills in school. We certainly weren't taught these skills by our parents. How could they teach us, when they themselves had never been taught?

In this last section of the book, we'll be looking at how to practise being assertive and more self-assured in various situations. We're going to be covering essentials, such as how to be acknowledged, heard and respected, how to let go of the need to please and rescue, how to say no, how to say 'Enough!' or 'I'm angry', as well as how to attract the right people into your life and know where you stand with them.

Once you have these tools, you'll see that leading an authentic and assertive life is an ongoing journey. These small acts of self-worth, these repeated and practised messages of your value mean that at some point you'll realise you've changed. You'll have stepped into your power.

So come with me now, and I'll give you some guidance. I'll teach you some tools, tips, and techniques so that you can learn to sail the ship of your own life, as I have done and so many of my clients have done before you.

Part Four

How Kind People Get Respect

Have you ever thought that other people appear to be so much more confident and resilient than you? Perhaps you feel that you're more sensitive than a lot of people, whether you show that or not.

The fact is that most of us are going through life looking at each other and thinking the same thing. We're all sensitive and vulnerable in our own ways, and we all think that others have a tougher skin than we do. That's why we can so easily hurt and offend each other, without any real awareness, or intention of doing so. It's also why we struggle and react defensively when we're on the receiving end of someone's disregard. It can feel so personal, and so painful!

When people think about assertiveness, respect is often what first comes to mind. But I've found that many people think about respect in the wrong way. They believe that respect is more about fending off disrespect than seeking respect. There's a fine line between the two. When we are disrespected, it's understandable that we might be tempted to tip the scales in the other direction. We want to be *looked up to*, rather than *looked down on*. But true respect has little to do with getting one's own back or raising oneself powerfully above another in order to feel better.

Rather than setting one person above another, true respect lifts everyone up to the same high level. It's a consciously kind way of being because it considers the value of everyone in the situation and seeks out solutions of mutual regard and worthiness.

Respect is something that we could all do with having in our lives, but it takes practice to become more self-assured and to let others know that you want their respect. It means setting and maintaining appropriate boundaries, practising great communication skills, and learning assertiveness techniques and methods that are relevant to different life situations. Focus on learning these, and you'll begin to feel more empowered and find it easier to ask for your needs to be met.

In the following three chapters we're going to be looking at practical everyday situations and scenarios where people tend to experience disrespect. I'll be highlighting the tools and strategies that can be a big help in gaining more respect in different relationships and situations.

Chapter 9
How to Be Acknowledged

Paula, 35

'There I was, waiting at the restaurant, and they'd never even told me they'd changed plans. It was like they'd just forgotten all about me!'

Paula was fed up with people always taking her for granted. Her friends just didn't seem to consider that she was a person with feelings. They'd let her down at the last minute or be rude to her without even realising what they were saying.

It was the same with her romantic relationships. At first, the men in her life would be so very attentive, giving her lots of consideration and respect, but soon they'd start to take her for granted or cancel dates at the last minute.

To Paula, it seemed like everyone she met ended up treating her with disregard and disrespect. At thirty-five, Paula was beginning to question if she was simply meeting the wrong people, or if it was something to do with how she herself was behaving in these relationships.

I admired Paula's insight. The fact that she was asking herself this question meant she was starting to take control of her life, to be more intentional and take responsibility for her own happiness.

When people take us for granted, it can be so easy to keep blaming them for doing so, but that won't change anything. Blaming can only lead to two unhelpful outcomes: stay in the relationship and remain unhappy, possibly moaning at the person, or walk away from them. A more helpful approach is to stop and consider:

'Am I giving out a signal that is encouraging them to behave this way?'

'Am I being intentional about my relationships or just expecting others to take responsibility for my happiness?'

The simple act of asking these questions is a good first step in breaking patterns of disrespect.

The Perils of 'Oh, I Don't Mind!'

Paula told me that she was always quite laid-back when she went out with friends and on dates. She enjoyed lots of different activities and so was content to fall in with what others wanted to do.

She certainly didn't want to be high maintenance, she told

me—that was a turn-off—and it just wasn't in her nature to be picky anyway.

It's quite common for people to just go along with what others want, sometimes because they don't want to come across as being fussy, sometimes because they simply don't have a preference.

So, when someone asks them to choose, they say:

'Oh, I don't mind, whatever you like.'

If this is you, maybe you genuinely don't mind. Perhaps you're a laid-back, easy-going person, who is just happy to be enjoying people's company and you really aren't that fussed about what the activity is, or the choice of restaurant, or the film or so on.

But what message does this convey? Could it be telling people that they don't have to stop to consider your choices, because, well, you don't really make any? You don't really care? And in time, how does that message grow in their subconscious? Are you signalling to them that you don't really care about other things either, such as if they are late, or forget to contact you? Someone may be the kindest, most lovely person on the planet, but if they don't have you at the front of their mind, they may well quite innocently forget about your needs, because you've been giving them the message that they don't need to see you as a priority.

If you've been an 'Oh, I don't mind' sort of person, it's time to start being more specific.

Quick Win

The next time someone offers you options, pick one! It's that easy. Even if you really don't mind if you see film A, B or C, select one. State clearly, 'I would like to watch film A,' or 'I would like to watch film B,' or 'I would like to watch film C.'

This is so powerful, because it:

- Gives a clear message to your subconscious that you're worthy and deserving of having your desires met
- Signals to the other person that you expect to be given attention and respect.

Here are some more examples.

You're in a restaurant and scanning the menu. Say:

'The … looks good. That is what I want.'

You're choosing a holiday destination. Say:

'I want to go to ... because I like ....'

Someone suggests the idea of going to see a play. Say:

'I want to see ... because I'm interested in ....'

Even though it may not matter to you what's on the menu, what your holiday destination is, or which play you see, what does matter is that you choose one. This is not being picky—it's practising how to be assertive so that it becomes a more natural habit for you.

These firm choices paint a very clear picture to others that you are a person who values themselves, is worthy of respect and regard and being given proper attention instead of being taken for granted.

This isn't to say that you must stick rigidly to your choice. For example, if everyone else prefers a different play, just go along with that and smile, saying, 'My turn to choose next time.'

Paula hadn't realised that, by being so laid-back, she was actually sending out the wrong signals. It was easy to blame people for forgetting about her needs, when she herself wasn't taking responsibility to get them met.

Once she decided to be more intentional, she began to feel more empowered. She began to have fun with this practice. She'd pick small things and be very clear about what she liked and didn't like. 'It makes me feel confident,' she told me.

Within a couple of weeks, her friends began to pay her more attention. They no longer took her for granted, they made sure to contact her and asked her opinion about things. It was amazing how this one small change in behaviour made such a huge difference in her relationships.

You Don't Always Have to go Head-On

There are times when it's necessary to come straight out and tell someone that their behaviour is upsetting you in some way—whether it's something they're doing, or not doing—and to firmly let them know that it's unacceptable.

It takes courage to stand up and be counted, and we often think, in situations like that, that we have to be quite abrupt and even somewhat forceful. But there may be situations where you don't have to go head-on. There are ways to get your message across in more subtle ways that still make the point clear.

Paula, for example, didn't confront her friends by demanding that they *must* respect her; instead she got her point across in a subtler and subliminal way by being more specific about her choices.

In some situations though, being outspoken doesn't feel appropriate. For example, with a superior at work. You may not want to rock the boat if you believe there's a lot at stake; you may even be worried that you might lose your job. While this is unlikely, it can still feel very scary to challenge someone in this position.

In this type of situation, a highly confident and assertive person would call a meeting and state their case. But what if you're not that highly confident and assertive person? Many people aren't.

Laura, 22

Laura had always wanted to work in fashion, so when she landed a trainee role with a popular magazine, she was thrilled. She knew she'd have to start from the bottom and work her way up, but she was willing to put in the hard work.

Wanting to make a good impression, Laura took on any task with good grace. No matter how menial or tiresome the task, she would put a smile on her face and say yes!

Her boss, Vicki, would often ask Laura to run errands, such as collecting items from other locations, sometimes more than an hour away. Laura would use her own car, and fuel, and drive across the city, often in hot, stuffy traffic, to pick things up for Vicki. On her return, Vicki would just grab the items from her without a word of thanks, and bark instructions to Laura about her next task.

As the weeks went by, Vicki's constant abruptness and taking her for granted was making Laura feel humiliated, small, and unworthy. She was beginning to lose her enthusiasm for the job—something she'd thought would never happen. She couldn't see a way forward. 'To be honest,' she told me, 'I'm a bit scared of Vicki—she's so serious and short with me—I actually feel a bit bullied by her.'

Laura didn't want to rock the boat and risk her job, but she couldn't go on feeling like she was being treated like a doormat. What was the answer?

Outlining

Outlining is a great way to pull someone's focus around without coming across as confrontational. To outline means to describe. As with all assertiveness techniques, it's a good idea to think first about what you want, and how you might say it. And because it's easy to come up with an idea and then forget it, it works best if you write those ideas down.

I'm a great advocate of using old-fashioned pen and paper because writing by hand encourages us to slow down; it helps us to focus on the right questions and their solutions. However, if you prefer typing notes into a device, go ahead. Just make sure you get the ideas down somewhere!

I suggested Laura try adding some outline to the words she would use when saying yes to one of Vicki's demands.

Here are some of the phrases that Laura came up with:

- 'Yes, sure, I'll collect that for you from [location].'
- 'Yes, of course I can get it, I'll use my car.'
- 'OK, I'll get the coffee from [location]. Just coffee, or do you want anything else?'
- 'Yes, I can do that, and I'll stop off for fuel on the way.'
- 'OK, it will take me about an hour to drive there and back.'

By adding some detail, Laura was prompting Vicki to focus more on all the hard work and effort that she was putting in.

This may seem like a simple concept, but it's an extremely powerful method for getting someone's full attention. Vicki, just like many of the people who can take us for granted, wasn't a monster. She was simply distracted and overwhelmed by her busy job.

Where previously Laura had been giving Vicki the message that she didn't mind being taken for granted, now these small additions to her verbal descriptions subtly encouraged Vicki to pay more attention.

Pretty soon, Vicki started to acknowledge the effort that Laura was making. In turn, Laura warmed to Vicki. It became a relationship of mutual regard and respect. After all, Laura could so easily have continued as they were, and complained about Vicki behind her back. That 'I'm Ok, You're not Ok' attitude, however, would have kept them stuck in a loop of resentment and misunderstanding.

Outlining is a subtle but powerful method. It's a way to communicate to someone that you require a little more respect and regard without having to confront them head-on. It can take a little practice, which is why it's worth writing your phrases down and practising them. I've made some suggestions to get you started in the worksheet called **The Subtle Practice Of Outlining**.

You can find this worksheet in the free companion course at the website www.howkindpeople.com

What Subconscious Deals Are You Making?

Laura had been so keen on being a success at her job, that quite without realising it, she'd set up a subconscious people-pleasing deal with Vicki. These subconscious deals, often called *psychological contracts*, are very common, especially in the workplace where there is a hierarchical structure in place. When people make these subconscious deals, they have no awareness that they're communicating a message about how they should be treated—and it's often done in a way that devalues their worth.

When we approach life from the belief that we have to please people, we are messaging: 'I'll always be there for you and make sure your needs are met. I won't expect you to think about my needs, because I think you're more important than I am. Then you'll like me and think I'm a good person and approve of me.'

It's important, then, to pay attention to how we communicate with people: not just in our words, tone, and body language, but also in our actions and how we treat ourselves.

Quick Win

If you are in a challenging situation with someone, ask yourself:

'When I do this, what message am I conveying to this person about how I expect to be treated?'

'Am I signalling to them that I am a person of worth, or am I signalling that I don't value myself?'

It was Laura's eagerness for the job that had started her off in a people-pleasing deal with Vicki. Once she saw this, she was able to consider how to change the message she'd been conveying. Now, by adding some description to the tasks she was completing—outlining them more clearly—she was communicating: 'Yes, I understand that you're my boss. I am willing to do a good job. I'm making it clearer that I'm doing so, and I expect you to take note of that and validate my hard work.'

It's Not the Thing Itself ...

When someone does something that leaves us feeling disregarded, it's often not the thing itself, but rather the meaning we attach to it, and the emotions it brings up for us. We're often not aware of this though, because we're more likely to be thinking about the actual event.

Take the example of someone who always turns up late. We'll communicate about that specific issue by moaning, 'You're always late, why can't you turn up on time!' In reality, did that person think to themselves, 'I know, I'll turn up late, just to make her feel taken for granted!' It's highly unlikely that they did (unless you have evidence that games are afoot, in which case run for the hills). They were probably simply distracted and completely unaware that their behaviour was disrespectful. So focusing purely on the event itself and getting cross doesn't really resolve the problem. Most likely, it will just lead to two people feeling bad: one hurt and disregarded, the other blamed and guilty.

The problem is that we *do* get cross because when someone disrespects us, it leaves us feeling powerless and small.

Emotionally, we time-travel back to some subconscious childhood hurt. The inclination then is to react to the current situation from our child self. We all do this, but it's not helpful.

So, whenever you feel disregarded in some way and you find yourself wanting to retaliate, ask yourself the following:

- 'What is the meaning that I am attaching to this person's behaviour?
- 'What are these feelings and emotions that I am experiencing?'
- 'In reality, did that person purposely set out to hurt and disrespect me?'

You can then more easily communicate from your adult self by letting the person know the meaning you attach to the event, and the feelings it brings up for you. This offers them an opportunity to see the bigger picture rather than feeling blamed, judged, and not good enough.

You could say something along the lines of: 'When you didn't turn up, I took it that you didn't care. I felt sad.' And *that* is a much more powerful message. It's an assertive way of communicating because it circumvents anger, blame, and control. As we've seen, we are wisdom-seekers by nature. We want to find solutions to challenges and move forward. Nobody wants to feel stuck in the role of baddie—sent down a dead-end road of blame and shame with no way out. So people need to not only understand if they've upset us in some way—they also need to be given some indication of how to make things better.

Nobody *Makes* You Feel

I think every one of us has at some point said to someone: 'You make me feel ...!' It's a natural phrase—but do try to avoid it if you can.

While a person's behaviour can indeed trigger an emotional response in us, no one actually *makes* us feel a certain way. I know, this one is hard to grasp, but in reality, your feelings are personal to you and are likely based on some other event from long ago. To say *you make me* is accusatory and will only lead to the other person being defensive. A more useful way to communicate this is something along the lines of:

'When ... happens, I find myself feeling ... .'

Or:

'It would help our relationship if you would be extra careful not to ... because that often brings up feelings of ... for me.'

You could substitute 'relationship' with 'friendship', 'business' etc.

You may like to write these two statements down. Then you'll have them ready. Rehearse them, and when the time is right, use them to help you have an authentic conversation with a more positive outcome.

Sum Up Points

- Being too easy-going and vague can convey the message that you don't expect others to consider your needs.
- Practising being more specific in your choices gives a subtle message that you deserve to be noticed.
- We make subconscious deals with people about how they should treat us by the way we treat ourselves.
- Being more assertive doesn't mean we have to be blunt—it can be communicated in subtle messages by, for example, describing more precisely the things we are doing for someone.
- Being clear on the meaning you attach to an event and the emotions it brings up for you, and then conveying that in a calm and adult manner can help a person see the bigger picture of a challenging situation.
- True respect doesn't set one person above another; rather, it lifts everyone up to the same high level.

Self-Reflective Questions for How to Be Acknowledged

1. What does being acknowledged mean for me personally?

2. In what ways can I respect myself so that others will respect me?

3. How can I be more specific and intentional about my choices?

In your **Intentional Life Plan,** you will find the template: **Being Acknowledged**. Consider these self-reflective questions and use your conclusions to help you complete it.

www.howkindpeople.com

Chapter 10
How to Be Heard

Felicity, 29

Felicity and her husband Mark had started an eCommerce business. It was doing well—or at least she thought it was. The problem was that Mark never consulted her about anything. He would just go ahead and make decisions. Often the first she heard of them was when it was too late to make changes.

Felicity and Mark had three small children under the age of five. What with the kids and the business, life could be stressful; but much as Felicity was grateful for Mark's hard work, she felt disregarded because he never seemed to consider her opinion.

'I've told him so many times, but he just doesn't listen,' she said to me. 'He says he'll consult with me, but then he just goes and ignores me again. Last week I discovered he'd invested a large sum of money on a new website design. I only found out when I went to the site and saw it had completely changed!

We've had some huge rows because I get so frustrated. Why won't he just listen to me!'

Everyone wants to be valued and respected. If that's not happening, we quite naturally want to talk about it, so that we can remedy the situation. But sometimes trying to talk about it can feel like talking to a brick wall. If you keep telling someone you're upset, and nothing ever changes, it can be frustrating and disheartening. Not only that, but you may even be accused of moaning and nagging, when all the time you're just trying to let them know that you're unhappy. All this can make you lose confidence in your own point of view and knowing where you stand.

To resolve differences of opinion, it's crucial to be heard. The problem is that people try to make themselves heard in all the wrong ways. This is partly because, well, none of us are born with a PhD in communication skills—we need to learn this stuff. It's also because we resort to ways we learnt when we were children, such as sulking, being defensive or emotional blackmailing. I'm sure you have done this on the odd occasion—we all do. It's natural; but it's not so helpful. When we can learn more adult ways to communicate our needs, it makes a huge difference in making sure we're being fully heard.

Expecting Different Results

There's an interesting quote, often attributed to Albert Einstein. It goes:

'The definition of insanity is doing the same thing over and over again but expecting different results.'

Well, much as I'm not calling anyone insane, I have to say that, especially with our relationships, a lot of us have a tendency to keep repeating the same thing over and over—in utter frustration. We say things like 'How many times do I have to tell you . . . !' (Clearly a few times hasn't done the trick, so how many times do we want to repeat ourselves?)

Felicity was utterly frustrated because Mark didn't seem to listen. Maybe this is a familiar experience for you? Have you had a situation where you keep trying to get your point across and the other person simply doesn't acknowledge you? Or worse still, maybe you've been told you're moaning and nagging, when all you're really trying to do is say, 'I'm feeling hurt and disrespected.'

In fact, if you could find the courage to make yourself vulnerable and actually say *those* words, you'd have a far better chance of being heard. Remember: being assertive is just as much about showing your vulnerability as it is about making it clear that you want respect.

Because Felicity kept on at Mark, all he heard was white noise.

He'd heard the same words so many times, they'd become meaningless to him. In his head he was probably thinking something like 'Oh, there's Felicity going on about this thing again. Honestly, I can't understand why she's making such a fuss. I'll just let her rant on until she runs out of steam.'

When one person is desperately asking to be heard, and the other is simply not listening, life becomes an unhappy deadlock. Yet, there is a remarkably easy way to remedy this.

'Don't Want' is Our Default Position

Human beings are hardwired to the negative. When we're unhappy about something, we tend to focus on just that—we talk about what we Don't Want.

'Don't Want' is our default position. It's normal to do this because it's human nature to focus on the negative first and then try to fix it. If your ancestor was being chased by a wild animal, he knew he *didn't want* to wait around to be eaten! So at a very basic level, there's nothing intrinsically wrong with the Don't Want attitude.

However, when it comes to our relationships, this attitude doesn't help—in fact, it tends to push people away and reinforce the problem rather than solving it. Clear, confident communication is all about positive signals and messages—not negative. Don't Want basically gives the message that the other person is at fault. It doesn't give them the opportunity to find a solution—instead, it comes across as blaming and shaming. And as I mentioned in the last chapter, 'How to Be Acknowledged', approaching from the perspective of what a person has done wrong is like leading them down a dead-end road.

So What Do You Actually *Want?*

On the other hand, giving someone a potential solution by suggesting what they can do is extremely empowering for them, and for you.

We all enjoy feeling connected and validated. So when we focus on positive outcomes, we draw others into that energy space with us; they feel good and are far more likely to respond in helpful ways. I've seen this happen so many times with my clients: when they ditch the Don't Want and adopt a more Do Want attitude in their relationships—well, life suddenly becomes a whole lot easier. They start to feel heard, at last!

So how can we achieve this? Let's go back to Felicity's experience.

When she was describing her frustration with Mark, Felicity gave me a big clue when she said, 'No matter how many times I tell him I'm fed up with being ignored…' I noticed that she was focusing on what she didn't want. She didn't want to be ignored.

There's a powerful difference between saying *I want* to be heard, and *I don't want* to be ignored. When someone hears what we *don't* want, they generally interpret it on a negative, emotional level. Here are some examples of those interpretations:

'You're not good enough.'

'It's all your fault.'

'I'm not sure how I feel about being in this relationship with you.'

'I'm just sending a lot of negativity and moaning your way because I'm annoyed.'

'Neither of us is in control of this situation.'

On the other hand, when a person hears about what we *do* want, they tend to interpret it on a positive emotional level as follows:

'You're good enough.'

'No one is at fault here.'

'I'm invested in our relationship.'

'This is something of importance.'

'We can manage this situation.'

It's remarkable how changing from the negative Don't Want to the positive Do Want can shift mountains. After all, an assertive approach to relationships is about positivity and love—not fear and scarcity!

Put like this, it seems an easy solution to swap from negative to positive. But because we're hardwired towards the negative, it can be surprisingly difficult to articulate what we do want in concise and considerate ways. Here are some steps to help you get better at this.

Step 1. Getting Clear

First, ask yourself the following question:

'If this is what I *don't* want, what is it that I *do* want?'

For Felicity, it was as follows:

'I *don't want* to be uninformed about the business; therefore, I *do want* to be informed about the business.'

Step 2. Offering a Solution

The next step is to consider any solutions that will help the person you're communicating with feel that they have the option for a positive outcome. Here are some examples:

'If you're going to be late, can you send me a quick text?'

'When you leave all the housework to me, I'll send you an email to remind you (Grin).'

We are all big kids at heart; we love to be made to feel that we're getting things right ... and that we're good enough. When you give people opportunities to feel that way, they'll be far more likely to hear you and attend to your needs than if you send them a barrage of don't wants!

Step 3. Emotional Needs

Once you've identified your *do want*, and have found a possible solution to suggest, the next step is to consider the emotional needs. We looked at these in 'How to Be Acknowledged' when we saw that letting someone know the meaning and the emotions behind an upset can greatly help in getting them to understand what the true problem is.

For Felicity, the emotional need was about worthiness. She felt that Mark hadn't informed her about the business because he didn't consider her worthy enough to share important information.

As Felicity explored this in our sessions, she realised that, since giving up work, she'd lost her sense of identity and her confidence. Mark was inadvertently making that worse by his apparent lack of attention.

Felicity began to change statements such as 'Mark, I'm fed up with you keeping things from me!' to 'Mark, I'd like you to keep me in the loop.' Then she added a possible solution, so that the next stage of the message became: 'Mark, I'd like you to keep me in the loop. Let's set aside a time each week so that you can update me on the business.' She then added a comment about the emotional need that would be fulfilled for her. This meant Mark would be able to not only find a practical solution, but also understand her emotions, making the communication so much more meaningful. Here is her message in its entirety.

'Mark, I'd like you to keep me in the loop. Let's set aside a time each week so that you can update me on the business. It will make a huge difference if you do that, because I'll feel more respected.'

It didn't take long for Mark to truly hear Felicity. He no longer experienced an angry barrage of white noise from her, because now she was being so clear.

This gave them space to properly communicate. The reality was that Mark would often keep things from Felicity because he could see that she had her hands full with the kids. He reminded her how much he admired her parenting skills; he was in awe of how she managed to care so well for their three children, all under the age of five. The last thing he wanted to do was add to her busy schedule, so he'd been taking on the load of the business to reduce her stress and to make sure he provided well for his family. He certainly didn't see her as unworthy!

I've provided a worksheet to help you define your Do Wants. It is called **One Powerful Way to Make Sure You're Heard.** You can find this worksheet in your companion course at the website

www.howkindpeople.com

Looking Through Their Lens

Susie, 37

Susie had a very high-pressure job in a business consultancy. She loved her work, but it meant long hours and a lot of travelling. Often Susie would get home exhausted. All she wanted to do was relax, but there would often be a ton of housework to do.

Her husband Martin would come in from his work, grab a coffee and sit in front of the TV. Whenever Susie asked him for help, he would be very attentive and help, but then, the next day he would be back to his old habits.

One evening Susie looked at the huge mountain of washing waiting to be ironed. She was about to call Martin to help but she sighed in exasperation. What was the point? So she stopped calling for help. But the resentment kept on building, which wasn't good for their relationship. Suzie felt completely stuck and frustrated.

In our session she told me, 'It's not that he doesn't care: he's actually really helpful. I'm just fed up having to keep asking him over and over. It's like he doesn't register that the task needs to be done without me pointing it out each time. And when I do ask, I feel like I'm constantly going on at him.'

It was confusing for Susie because clearly Martin was a willing helper, but he didn't seem to understand how important it was to offer without having to be asked.

It can be very frustrating when someone doesn't seem to understand our point of view. But given that being truly assertive is about finding a positive, win-win, outcome, it's not helpful to assume that others must see the world as we do. It's far more helpful to consider the lens through which they view the world and try communicating with them from that perspective. It gives them a better chance to hear the message.

I asked Susie to tell me more about Martin. I learnt that he was a graphic designer, and that life was a lot of fun with him - they were mainly very happy. 'He has a great sense of humour,' she said. 'In fact, he can be a bit of a big kid really, and that's charming, but it means I have to be the grown-up all the time.'

I suggested that Suzie try to take a more creative and light-hearted approach. So the next time there was a big pile of washing, she took a photo of it and sent it in a message to him with the phrase: 'Emergency: Mount Washing Erupts Again! Rescue Services Needed'.

Given his personality, the picture and the humour had much more of an impact on Martin than Susie simply talking at him in a serious manner. Susie realised that they had formed a dynamic—a pattern of him waiting for her to nag, and when she did, it became the signal that it was time for him to take action. However, once she started considering his approach to life, and adapting her message accordingly, he began to hear her. It was much easier for him to take responsibility for his share of the housework because it had become part of his world.

If you're struggling to be heard by someone who isn't quite getting it, it's no one's fault; it's likely that it's all getting lost in translation. You can be more intentional about how you handle this by taking responsibility for how you're communicating with them.

We can get even more intentional, and specific, about communicating with someone from their perspective by using a technique drawn from Neuro Linguistic Programming (NLP).

NLP sees each of us as having an inner representational

system of the world. We make sense of information using certain internal representations. I call these language styles.

These are:

- Visual
- Auditory
- Kinaesthetic
- Auditory Digital (Self-Talk)
- Gustatory
- Olfactory

Let me give you some examples:

A person who thinks in images will tend to use more visual words. They will say things like:

'I can see where you're coming from.'

'It looks like ...'

A person whose thoughts are focused on sounds will tend to use more auditory words. They will say things like:

'It sounds like ...'

'On another note, ...'

A person whose thoughts are based around feelings will tend to use words that are kinaesthetic. They will say things like:

'I'll get in touch with you.'

'I can't quite grasp what you mean.'

A person whose thoughts are based on Auditory Digital (Self-Talk) will tend to use words related to steps, procedures, and sequences. These are more system thinkers than sensory thinkers. They will say things like:

'What's the next step?'

'It doesn't add up!'

The above four are the most common language styles. There are two more: Gustatory (taste) and Olfactory (smell). Examples of Gustatory are:

'It's not to my taste.'

'It was a bittersweet experience.'

Examples of Olfactory are:

'I smell a rat!'

'Something's fishy about that.'

(It's worth noting that we use all of these language styles depending on the circumstances we find ourselves in. However, in the main, we stick to one or two.)

No matter how well intentioned you are, if you and another person are speaking in different language styles, you may just as well be speaking two different languages! It's not that you don't want to truly hear each other—it's that you simply can't!

So, the trick then is to identify the language style that a person is using and align your communication with theirs. I'm not suggesting you try to change your own style—that wouldn't work because it is your natural way of communicating. However, making small adjustments for important conversations can make all the difference.

I've provided a worksheet to help you with this. It is called **Language Styles Match The Words Game**. You can find this worksheet in your companion course at the website

www.howkindpeople.com

It's well worth completing this, as it's an easy way to learn how to notice language styles.

Sum Up Points

- Ask for what you do want, instead of focusing on what you don't.
- Identify the lens through which a person views the world and communicate from that perspective (i.e., sense of humour, being creative).
- Identify the person's specific language style and match yours to it when the topic is important.

- Try not to blame the other person—you're seeking a win-win outcome, not a right and a wrong one.
- Be clear on the meaning you and the other person are attaching to the situation.

Self-Reflective Questions for How to Be Heard

1. What areas of my life do I need to get clearer on what I *do* want?
2. What phrases can I use to tell people what I *do* want instead of what I *don't*?
3. How can I make sure to seek a win-win situation when things are challenging?
4. What is my language style?

In your **Intentional Life Plan**, you will find the template: **Being Heard**. Consider these self-reflective questions and use your conclusions to help you complete it.

www.howkindpeople.com

Chapter 11
How to Reclaim Your Time

Beth, 47

Beth was having a problem with her daughter, Emma, twenty-four. She had brought up Emma and her twin brother Daniel by herself and they'd been a tight family unit. They still were, even though Emma and Daniel had now grown up and flown the nest. Much as Beth missed their company, she also recognised that it was an opportunity for her to take some time for herself.

Whilst Daniel was very independent, Emma was just the opposite. She would call her mother, sometimes several times a day, and spend hours on the phone talking about all her life's worries. The situation was beginning to weigh on Beth.

She wanted to be there for her daughter, of course—but Beth was beginning to recognise that her urge to respond to Emma's needs wasn't just a mother thing. It was also much to do with her feelings of guilt. She felt guilty because she felt so bad about the kids growing up without their father. Even though it had been his choice to disappear, she still felt huge regret about the whole situation.

So, when Emma called and wanted Beth to spend hours on the phone, Beth felt compelled to be there for her. ‘It’s like compensation,’ she told me. ‘I feel like I have to give my time to recompense her for the time she lost with her father.’

To add to this, whenever there was tension between her and Emma, Emma would bring up the subject of her absent father and accuse Beth of having made terrible parenting mistakes.

Despite her feelings of guilt, Beth was growing tired of having to be there for Emma’s every whim. She was beginning to feel resentful that her newfound freedom was being stolen from her. Something needed to change.

From the way Beth talked about Emma, I could see that, despite their issues, there was much love between mother and daughter. However, the unhelpful dynamic needed to shift—Beth’s misplaced empathy wasn’t serving either of them.

If you ever have an issue that keeps repeating in a relationship, it’s likely that there’s some type of unhelpful dynamic happening. An unhelpful dynamic is where there is a pattern of behaviour going on between two people, where each reinforces the difficult behaviour in the other.

Beth’s guilt led her to overcompensate by always being there for Emma. Subliminally, this gave Emma the message that she herself couldn't cope; she felt hopeless and helpless, so she leant even more on Beth, which only served to reinforce Beth's guilt.

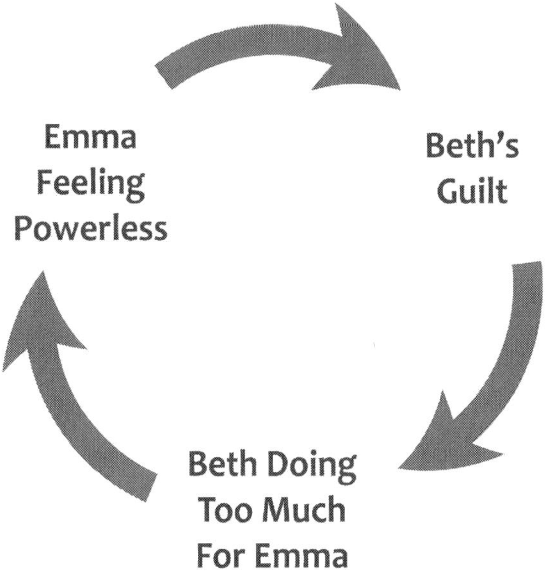

These hidden cycles can be very powerful; they'll go on forever until someone recognises the pattern and does something to break it. By not being authentic with Emma about her need for time and space, and being driven by guilt, Beth was keeping the cycle going.

Beth had had some inkling that always being available for Emma wasn't really helping, and she had tried to be more assertive with her in the past. On occasion she had messaged Emma saying she was too busy to talk, or she'd just avoided answering the phone altogether. However, the result was that Emma had gone into child mode, stamped her metaphorical foot, and accused Beth of all the times she'd let her down.

Emma didn't mean to be so ill-tempered. She was generally a lovely and kind person; but she was being driven by fear, panicking because she truly believed she needed her mother to rescue her.

When Beth and I explored her struggle to be more assertive with Emma, she realised that by ignoring Emma's calls or telling her she was too busy to talk, she hadn't been setting healthy boundaries at all—actually, she'd been putting up barriers. It can happen this way: when someone is feeling taken advantage of, they'll sometimes go too far the other way and put up barriers in order to reclaim their time, and space. This just leaves the recipient feeling confused and rejected. The solution for Beth was to reclaim her time in a way that offered them both love, kindness, and respect.

She could see now that her options were not about giving Emma *all* her time, or choosing to give *much less* of her time. Rather, her responsibility was to hold stronger boundaries *around* time. This would be a more consciously kind way to respond to Emma; it would encourage her to be more resilient and confident. In the long run, being assertive in this way would mean that she and Emma would each have an opportunity to grow as people—a win-win, instead of the lose-lose that it had been.

Time Boundaries

The fact is that people don't really steal our time from us—we give it away. And reclaiming our time can be challenging. If you feel like someone is stealing your time, simply ignoring them or saying, 'Stop bothering me, I'm busy!' is a barrier. It's not assertive. It's antagonistic. It just adds more disrespect to the situation because it disrespects the other person too.

The very best way to reclaim your time is to use time itself as a solution.

Setting boundaries around time works very well. It's a way of being intentional—it means pre-planning, instead of just reacting to what others want from you in the moment. It also means everyone is respected.

You can make a start on using these boundaries, by getting into the habit of saying yes, but within your own time frame. For example: 'Yes, I can do that, I'm free on Thursday.' This will help you let go of the sense of constant obligation to others whilst still feeling like you're being kind and considerate. As with so many of the methods in this book, this is very simple and easy to put into practice, yet it will create a powerful shift in your confidence, and in your relationships.

Beth came up with a plan to set some boundaries around Emma's constant and lengthy phone calls. The first thing she needed to do was give Emma a clear message that she only had a certain amount of free time to talk.

It wasn't really Emma's fault that she was claiming so much of her mother's time. The very fact that Beth had been allowing this to happen had been giving all the wrong signals to Emma. Beth needed to help Emma understand that she valued her own time. She came up with some phrases, ready to say to Emma the next time she got in contact, wanting a long chat. She wrote them down so she could see them in case she got flustered.

Here they are:

For a text message: I missed your call. I'm caught up now but I'm free at 6, I'll call you back then.

For a phone call: Hi darling, I'm free now for twenty minutes, then I have to go out, so do you want to chat until then, or would you rather call back later?

For an email: I always enjoy having a catch up with you, you know how much I love you. I have every faith in you being able to sort out that problem: I'm so proud of all you do in your life. I'm free tomorrow morning after 10 if you want to call and give me an update.

There were a few awkward moments at first, but soon Emma fell in with Beth's new boundaries. There had been no need for Beth to make great protestations about Emma taking up too much of her time. Emma became a lot happier in herself;

her confidence grew as she learnt to be more resilient, knowing that her mother would always be there for her—within respectful limits.

Now when they chatted, Beth really enjoyed the conversation rather than having the former niggling feeling of resentment. As their relationship became one of adult to adult, Beth was able to have a frank discussion with Emma about the past and her parenting. She was able to allow herself to be vulnerable with her daughter. Ultimately it was far more empowering than when she'd been reacting from a place of fear, constantly trying to smooth things over. In turn, Emma saw that she had been projecting her anger at her father onto her mother.

As you can see, respect isn't always necessarily about being extra nice to someone—it's about acknowledging that they have a life of real value. They deserve to be given the opportunity to learn and grow. For example, if we allow someone to treat us with disregard, not only are we disrespecting ourselves, but we're not respecting their right as a human being to reach their potential. Respect then, can sometimes require a little tough love. It's a delicate balancing act!

Hannah, 52

Since Hannah's uncle had passed away two years previously, Hannah had been spending a great deal of time with her elderly aunt Masie. Masie had been feeling very lonely, and Hannah was doing her best to be there for her.

The problem was that Masie was becoming more and more demanding of Hannah's time. Hannah felt that things were getting out of control. It was as though Masie wanted to monopolise her every moment.

'She gets so upset,' she said. 'Even if I have coffee with a friend, she gets jealous and accuses me of not caring about her. The only time I get to myself is when I'm at work—and that's not really free time. I can't seem to get her to understand that I just need some time for myself.'

Hannah was becoming ever more tired and resentful of the situation. She had tried to hide her feelings from Masie, she told me, but she knew that her aunt was picking up on her resentment. I could see that an unhelpful dynamic had formed.

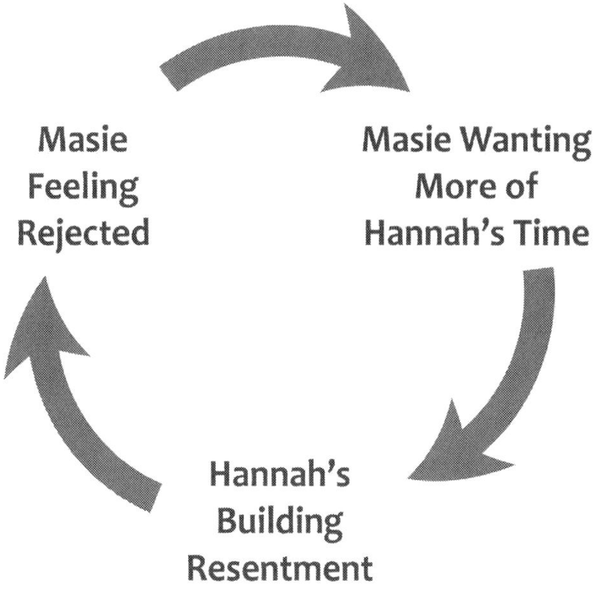

From Hannah's description of her aunt's behaviour, it would have been very easy to jump to the conclusion that Masie was just a selfish woman who didn't care about anyone else's needs but her own. Judgements though, never help. I was interested to find out more about Hannah and her aunt.

Hannah described herself as being an introvert—she needed time alone to recharge from the energy of other people and the busyness of life. On the other hand, she realised that Masie was more of an extrovert; she craved social interaction and stimulation.

For those people who need solitude, it can be extremely stressful to have someone constantly monopolising their time. And for those who need social interaction, it can feel like a painful abandonment when someone simply wants time alone. As we explored this, Hannah was able to consider that she and her aunt simply had different needs. This understanding allowed her to step back from the emotional intensity of the situation so that she could discuss it with Masie calmly and with kindness.

Masie was of a generation that wasn't familiar with the concept of the introvert personality; she hadn't understood Hannah's need for solitude. Once Hannah explained, Masie realised that Hannah wasn't abandoning or rejecting her. Now that they had some clarity, they were able to make a shift towards resolving the problem.

Instead of feeling plagued by her aunt's demands and feeling guilty and resentful, Hannah came up with some clear time boundaries. She arranged specific times in the week when she would visit and spend time with her aunt. Safe in the knowledge that this would definitely happen, her aunt calmed down. They began to enjoy each other's company much more. Hannah also found a social group for her aunt where she could make friends with people of her own age group so that she wouldn't be lonely in between Hannah's visits.

When Hannah had first started spending more time with her aunt, she'd done it with great kindness—but it had been a misguided type of kindness. At the time, she hadn't thought through the message that it would give her aunt: ‘I’m always available/but then maybe I’m not …’

Hannah found it much easier to be with her aunt because she was being clearer on what time she had available and setting boundaries around that. Now, she was focusing on what she did want, instead of feeling resentful about what she didn’t. She was being more authentic about her own needs and at the same time seeking a win-win outcome for them both.

Robina, 23 and Jo, 22

Robina had a thing about timekeeping. Her friend Jo did not. Every time they met for coffee, Jo would turn up at least twenty minutes late. As the minutes ticked by, Robina would grow steadily more frustrated, humiliated, and hurt.

‘I sit there getting worked up’, she told me. ‘I’m thinking that Jo thinks so little of me that she can’t be bothered. She doesn’t care about our friendship. By the time she arrives, I’m in such a foul mood that I end up snapping at her, and then later I feel embarrassed about being so rude. I wonder if I’m just being oversensitive.’

Whether Robina was being overly sensitive or not, the fact was that Jo’s constant lateness *did* annoy her. We can get so caught up with trying to decide if we are justified in our feelings, that we forget that *what we feel, is what we feel*—and that is OK. Clearly Robina was feeling disrespected.

I asked her what meaning she attached to Jo's lateness. Robina realised that much of the stress was due to having to sit there, feeling powerless, wondering what was happening. We explored ways that she could feel more empowered by taking responsibility for her part in the situation—after all, annoying as Jo's tardiness was, she wasn't physically forcing Robina to sit around and wait for her.

She decided to be more intentional by asking Jo to always message her when she was running late. She also decided that she would set a clear personal time boundary with Jo—she would never wait for her for more than thirty minutes. That way the stress would be reduced because she would always know where she stood.

Having these clear boundaries in place made it much easier for Robina to have a calm and kind conversation with Jo. The reality was that Jo had always been a terrible timekeeper. She was inclined to get distracted easily and would often get side-tracked by something just as she was leaving the house. She certainly didn't mean any disrespect to Robina.

Because Jo now understood how important it was to Robina and to their relationship, she made a real effort to curb her tardiness. As Robina relaxed about the situation, she came to accept that Jo was simply not good at timekeeping. She could let go of her frustration about the occasional late arrival because she no longer took it as a personal insult.

If possible, it's a very good idea to get into the habit of using time boundaries from the very beginning of any arrangement. That way, you can avoid sliding into giving all your time away, and then having to struggle to reclaim it. It's a way of preventing stress and respecting everyone concerned.

Some Time Boundary Phrases

Quick Win

'I'd love to help you, but I'm busy right now. But I do have a couple of hours on [day]. I can help you then.'

'I look forward to visiting you on [day], when I will have more time to relax with you.'

'Good to hear from you. Just to let you know I only have 5 minutes to talk right now—shall we arrange a time for a longer chat later on?'

'Would you like to come for dinner? Please let me know by [# time] so that I can make arrangements.'

'If you're going to be late, will you text me? I don't want to get all grumpy with you because I've been waiting around feeling anxious!'

We're all different. Some people have the type of lifestyle where they only know their schedule at the last minute; others have a more appointment-based schedule where they need to plan ahead. It's useful to remember that time is an individual experience; other people may not understand your particular time needs because theirs are different—and that's all the more reason to set some effective and clear boundaries.

If you offer your time, it is best to give it wholeheartedly and with grace. If you can't offer it, be clear on that: that's a consciously kind way of being which respects you, and the other person.

Sum Up Points

- People pick up on each other's emotional energy. They'll know if you're feeling resentful, so it's better to be authentic about the time you have available.
- Giving away all your time is a misguided kindness. It doesn't help the other person to be more responsible.
- People don't really steal your time—you give it away by not saying no.
- Putting up barriers by ignoring people or telling them you're unavailable doesn't help.

- Creating time boundaries is a highly effective way to claim your own time yet still respect others.

Self-Reflective Questions for How to Reclaim Your Time

1. What areas of my life do I currently want to make a priority?
2. How can I make this more clear to others?
3. What type of phrases can I use?
4. What am I grateful for?

In your **Intentional Life Plan**, you will find the template: **Reclaiming Time**. Consider these self-reflective questions and use your conclusions to help you complete it.

www.howkindpeople.com

Part Five

How Kind People Speak Their Truth

You know those people who always seem to know the right thing to say at the right time? They weren't made that way. It's likely they've learnt tools and techniques which have helped them become confident and assertive over time.

Learning to communicate effectively is a very important part of becoming more assertive. When emotions hold us hostage, the right words and actions can be elusive. If we have some communication skills already in place, it becomes so much easier to get the right message across, whether that's with our words or our actions.

People often wait a long while as they try to find the right time to say what needs to be said, and even when they do find that time, they still keep backing out. Speaking up and speaking our truth can seem daunting, because in order to do so we need to make ourselves vulnerable—there's the fear that we'll invite conflict, push people away, or be rejected. However, when we summon the courage to take action, our relationships become ever closer because love comes in and fear recedes.

Chapter 12
How to Say No

Max, 54

Max, a self-employed web developer, absolutely loved his work. However, he would often end up working long hours, fixing issues on people's websites—and all too often for a ridiculously low fee.

The problem was that whenever someone asked Max for a discount, he just couldn't bring himself to say no. The more he gave away his services for such little recompense, the more people would recommend him to their friends. All this pressure on his time and his finances had led to Max becoming increasingly stressed. He knew he needed to take responsibility to make his business work *for* him instead of against him.

I wondered what lay behind Max's struggle with saying no. When I asked him, he told me that he didn't want to be unkind. He thought that if he insisted on people paying the full fees for his services, he might come across as mean. He also feared that people would get annoyed and walk away, leaving him with no work at all.

Max's need to be kind was a misguided type of kindness. Ultimately, he wasn't being kind to anyone, because running his business into the ground would eventually lead to him not being able to help anyone. Clearly, Max had some limiting beliefs about money and self-worth.

As we explored this, Max told me that when he was nine years old, his father walked out, leaving him and his mother with no financial support. His mother was under a great deal of stress; she didn't handle money very well, and so Max did odd jobs to help contribute. Every day he cleaned cars, walked people's dogs, did paper rounds—anything to bring money into the household. Whenever young Max tried to say no to his mother's requests for him to do extra work, she'd get upset and accuse him of not caring about her. Max recalled many times when he was exhausted by all the chores, on top of school. Eventually, he fell behind with his schoolwork and never truly caught up—a reason he so valued the tech skills he'd managed to pick up along the way.

Up until our sessions, Max hadn't seen the link between how life had been way back in his childhood, and how he thought about his business today. He saw now that he'd grown up with some very unhelpful ideas about how earning money and self-worth went together.

It was a lightbulb moment. Max began to consider the possibility that he didn't have to listen to that anxious little boy who'd been so worried about being seen as uncaring.

Like many of us, Max had been so concerned about what others would think of him that it was getting in the way of him asking for his basic needs to be met. When we worry and fret about how we'll come across to others, we put so much attention on ourselves that fear builds. I suggested to Max that he spend some time researching other IT specialists to find out about their services. He saw the prices they were charging, and he realised that he wasn't thinking of these people as mean or unkind. He concluded that charging for the high value of his own work wouldn't be unkind or arrogant. It was simply a fair exchange in an adult world.

Let the Contract Say it For You

I also encouraged Max to take a free business course run by the local authorities. On the course, he learnt how to create a formal contract to set out his fees and services more clearly.

As we've seen, to be assertive, we need to be very clear; that way everyone knows where they stand in a situation. If services, fees, and conditions are clearly stated in a written piece of content, then there are no grey areas left to argue about personal opinions and differences, and far less likelihood that emotions will get in the way.

Contracts don't just have to be for business though; they can be used in all sorts of situations. Your **Intentional Life Plan,** for example, is your own contract with yourself. It's your personal guide for how you will lead a more assertive life—something to refer to.

Popping into Child

Like Max, many people struggle with saying no because of the experiences they had in their early childhood. If always saying yes meant that Mummy, or the teacher, wouldn't be cross with you—well, that was a good thing. So it became a learnt habit.

That habit can be hard to break, but it is perfectly possible. I've seen many people learn to say no—it just takes a little practice. A good start is to recognise when you're coming from your child self, and to deal with the emotions associated with that.

First, please do remember that there's absolutely nothing wrong with popping into child—we all do it, often several times a day. It's no big deal. However, when you get into one of those 'I want to say no but I keep saying yes—aaagh!' situations, it's very empowering to notice whether you're coming from your worried, inner child's perspective or not, and if you are, then to remind yourself that in the grown-up world, it's perfectly OK for adults to say no to each other.

And if, when you say no to someone, they have a little tantrum, that's because they themselves have likely popped into *their* own child self. There's no point in getting into an argument—just give them a bit of time to calm down and come to terms with your 'no'.

Yes, No, and Emotions

As I mentioned in chapter 7 'When Emotions Hold Us Hostage', in the many years I've been helping people learn to be more assertive I've seen that there are three common emotions which cause a problem. They are fear, guilt, and resentment.

These three each have their own role in the Yes/No struggle. It's quite likely they'll be familiar for you.

- If I say no, I feel guilty.
- If I say no, I feel fear.
- If I say yes, I feel resentment.

Let's take a moment to explore these and find ways to manage them from a more adult and assertive perspective.

Guilt

Adrian, 47

Adrian happily admitted that he spoiled his daughter Fiona. She wrapped him around her little finger; all she had to do was ask and he'd give her anything she wanted. In return, she doted on her dad.

Now Adrian was having some financial problems and had to tighten his belt. However, Fiona had been invited on an expensive skiing trip with her friends and she expected that Dad would fund it for her. 'I just feel so guilty when I think about telling her that I'm not going to pay for it. I'm considering taking out a loan to cover it,' he confided in me.

Adrian's guilt came from the fact that he spent a great deal of time away from home due to his work. He had developed a habit of justifying the time he spent on his business, by financially compensating the family. As we explored this, Adrian came to see that giving Fiona everything she wanted was a misguided type of kindness: a quick fix to alleviate his own guilt.

To be consciously kind, he needed to look at the bigger picture. Saying no to Fiona would help her better understand the value of money and prepare her for her future. It also meant he could be his authentic self instead of constantly trying to be her superhero, which he admitted was a strain at times. He recognised that putting up with some short-term feelings of guilt about Fiona's skiing trip was kinder to her because it would help her mature. As he went through this process, he could see that he himself was growing as a person because he was parenting better, and Fiona was growing as a person because she was learning to become independent.

Fear

Natalie, 19

On Saturday nights, Natalie and her friends would go to a local bar. There was always extremely loud music playing. Natalie had very sensitive hearing and she found it a real challenge; she'd often end up with a headache. She feared that if she told her friends she wanted to go somewhere else, they would abandon her.

As we explored this, Natalie realised that by saying nothing just to keep the peace, she wasn't being truly authentic with her friends, or even consciously kind to herself. It was time to overcome her fear, and speak up.

When she did, nothing bad happened—they compromised. Her friends agreed to go to a different venue with her sometimes and understood that if they went to the noisy bar she wouldn't attend. On reflection, Natalie realised that had they dropped her, they wouldn't have been such good friends anyway.

Taking the risk of removing her mask and being her true self took courage, but ultimately it did a lot for Natalie's confidence. It bonded her with her friends because they were seeing the real her. It gave them an opportunity to show the kind and caring side of their nature. It also gave all of them the opportunity for self-reflection and to grow and mature a little more. It was a win-win, 'we're all OK' outcome.

Resentment

Julie, 34

Julie's younger sister Amy had been born with some heart problems. Several operations in her childhood meant that Amy was now a healthy and fit young woman with a bright future ahead of her.

However, those childhood years had taken their toll on all the family. Julie was only twelve when Amy was born, and from that time on, she was cast in the role of carer—often with her own needs being pushed aside. It was no one's fault: it was just how life had to be.

Julie did love her sister, but even now, there was always something stressful going on for Amy—and there seemed to be an expectation that Julie would always be willing to drop everything to attend to her sister's wishes.

It's quite common to see this dynamic within families: everybody sees the other in a certain role, and there's the assumption that each will continue to act accordingly. Those roles, however, often become completely outdated as life has moved on and situations have changed.

Julie was beginning to feel ever more frustrated as the years went on. The problem was that her efforts to be kind and caring to Amy meant that the word 'yes' would come out of her mouth automatically. Later on, she'd regret it, and feel resentful because her own needs had been put aside, yet again.

In our sessions, Julie came to see that there was a pattern going on—a dynamic between herself and Amy for which she was just as much responsible as her sister. This was a huge insight for her as she recognised that she was replaying an old role.

She began to notice that Amy was often much more capable and resilient about situations than she'd been assuming. Instead of dropping everything and rushing to help her sister, she began acknowledging Amy's strengths and telling her how proud she was of her. Their dynamic changed from an I'm Ok, You're Not OK imbalance, to a much more adult and supportive friendship.

The Body Doesn't Lie

I wonder if you can relate to Julie's experience: agreeing to something, and then later wishing that you hadn't been so quick to give away your time and energy?

The fact is that we usually know in the moment if we really want to say no to a request. Even if we can't get clear in our mind, we can physically feel the resistance: we'll feel tense. The body doesn't lie—it will say a clear no, even if we're struggling to speak up.

So do listen to your emotions. If they are urging you to say no, but you're struggling, ask yourself the following questions:

Quick Win

'Is avoiding unpleasant feelings such as guilt or fear more important to me than this relationship?'

'Can I speak my truth and sit with the discomfort of these feelings for a while?'

'If I say yes, then feel resentful, is that helpful for my relationship?'

As I mentioned earlier, a lot of communication happens via the subtle messages we pass to each other. Most people are good at reading body language; even if it's only on an unconscious level, they'll be able to tell if you're not being authentic.

The kindest thing you can do for relationships is to take a little courage to speak your truth by mastering the art of saying no. Here are some ways to begin:

How to Say No: 6 Easy Ways

1. Stop telling yourself that you can't say no

If you keep telling yourself something, it reinforces the belief. Next time you catch yourself saying, or thinking, 'I'm not good at saying no,' try this:

First, don't try to push that thought away, because resisting it will only make it stronger. Instead, notice the thought and follow it up with something like 'Up until now I haven't been good at saying no, but I'm learning to get better at it.'

2. Delay

Use a delay tactic. Very rarely does a request require an answer there and then.

Delay statement examples:

'I'm not sure about that. I'll check my diary and come back to you as soon as I can.'

'I don't want to say yes and then let you down, so let me think about it. I'll let you know tomorrow.'

If someone is pressuring you for an immediate answer, it's very likely because they're feeling pressured themselves. A good tactic is to say something like 'Gosh, it sounds urgent for you.' This will steer them towards a clearer explanation about the issue and give you space to consider it.

3. Avoid Vague Messages

Avoid using vague words because that will convey an unclear message. Words like 'Um', 'Ah', 'Maybe', 'Perhaps', 'Not Sure' convey a message that it could be a 'yes', just as much as a 'no'. It's not fair to the other person to mislead them.

4. Give Them a Potential Solution

If you are saying 'no', can you offer the person an alternative? It could be something along the lines of:

'I can't help, but maybe [name of person] could help you?'

'It's just not my sort of thing, but I know [name of person] is interested in that.'

'I'd rather do …. How do you feel about that?'

5. Shut up!

Sometimes communication is simply about handing someone a message. Full stop. They may come back with an opposing point of view, but letting go of the need to engage in conversation about the situation is *very* powerful indeed. If you're clear in your mind about what you want to say, you only really need to say it once or possibly twice.

If you keep saying the same thing over and over, the other person just hears nagging and white noise. So just say what you need to say, and then shut up!

6. Transferable No's

If you find it difficult to say no to a specific person, or in specific situations, start a practice of saying no to smaller things.

I'm not suggesting you stubbornly say no to every little request, but consider those times when you automatically say yes where you could say no. Practise your small no's and your subconscious will get used to the idea that saying no is an OK and normal thing to do. It will also prepare others for the more challenging no's.

You'll find a handy worksheet: **Master the Art of Saying No** plus a guide on **Empowering Words and Phrases** in the free companion course www.howkindpeople.com

Sum Up Points

- Having your own clear and personal guidelines, which include your values and boundaries, gives you a great way to start putting 'saying no' into practice. It means the contract says it for you.
- Struggling to say no very often begins in childhood because children want to please their caregivers and avoid conflict.
- You can learn to overcome the 'say yes' habit by taking note of whether you're coming from your child-self or your adult-self.
- Having a loving word with your inner child will help to let go of the fear of saying no.
- It's actually a kind thing to say no to others, because it helps them become more resilient and confident. It also encourages them to be more confident in saying no to others
- Learning to say no is one of the most powerful things you can do to create confidence. Practise a little at a time and you'll find it becomes a natural part of your life.

Self-Reflective Questions for How to Say No

1. How would my relationships improve if I got better at saying no?
2. Which other areas of my life would improve?
3. How will learning to say no serve me, and others?

In your **Intentional Life Plan,** you will find the template: **Saying No**. Consider these self-reflective questions and use your conclusions to help you complete it.

www.howkindpeople.com

Chapter 13
How to Say 'I'm Angry'

I have to smile, as I recall myself many years ago, on a counselling training course. The subject of anger came up, and I said in all sincerity,

'Oh I don't do anger.'

At that time, I truly believed that *I don't do anger* was a good thing. Like so many people, I'd learnt to sidestep it, believing it to be something bad. I had yet to learn that it isn't anger itself that's the problem, but the way we express it.

A lot of people try to avoid anger because they associate it with hostility and aggression. That's hardly surprising because many of us have witnessed anger in just this way. Nobody wants to come across as unkind and confrontational. Maybe you've had similar concerns.

Like all emotions, anger is an energy, and all energy needs to find a way to express itself. If you try to avoid it, it will eventually find its own way out. People can hold on for ages, and then erupt. Or they can be passive-aggressive—

negativity leaking out as they play mind games, make barbed comments, embarrass people in front of others, put people down—all under the guise of some innocent remark or behaviour. Sometimes people turn anger in on themselves, having constant negative self-critical thoughts, which can lead to anxiety and depression.

Trying to keep the lid on anger also means we're never really being our authentic self, because people do, of course, make us angry sometimes. It's just the way things are in a world where we're all muddling along together. With our own individual belief systems and values, we're bound to bump up against each other sometimes. The important thing to remember is that it's not about being angry—it's about finding the best ways to express it.

Jake, 30 and Sandra, 32

Jake and Sandra came to me for couples therapy. They had a few issues to resolve, the most pressing of which was Jake's unmanageable anger. Sandra had threatened to end their marriage if he didn't learn to curb his temper. 'He's been so aggressive lately,' said Sandra, 'and now the children are becoming frightened of him.'

The couple had been under a lot of stress over the past year. Sandra was at home with their young children, so Jake was the sole provider for the family. Money was tight.

As we explored the triggers behind Jake's outbursts, a pattern emerged. It seemed that Jake would become very defensive when Sandra questioned him about domestic tasks that needed to be done. 'The other day he flew into a rage because I asked if he was going to fix the kitchen cupboard. Honestly, I'm scared to say anything in case he takes it the wrong way!'

Jake was also highly sensitive and would become very uptight if he thought Sandra was teasing him or belittling him in some way. I wondered why these particular things were triggering Jake's temper, and I asked him if he could remember feeling like this in the past.

The first thing that came to mind was his school years, which he described as 'a long stretch of misery'. Jake had dyslexia which hadn't been diagnosed until he was thirteen—he had spent much of his time struggling with schoolwork. He had got so far behind, that he had to repeat a year. The other children would bully him, and his older siblings would tease him, calling him Stupid Jake!

The dyslexia diagnosis was a turning point for Jake. He was given extra support at school, and he did very well, going on to get reasonable grades.

Jake's later achievements, however, could not dispel his deep-rooted childhood fear of being found out to be stupid. Each time Sandra teased him, or asked him to do some chore, he became that anxious little boy again—worried that he might, yet again, be exposed as inadequate.

Leaping to the End of the Fuse

Because anger is often felt so intensely, we tend to think of it as one big powerful emotion that stands all by itself. Anger, though, is really a secondary emotion. That is, it's an emotional *reaction* to other negative emotions the person is feeling. The most common of these are: hurt, humiliation, fear, frustration, and rejection.

When we express anger in inappropriate ways, such as temper and aggression, it's because we haven't noticed these other emotions: we've jumped straight to the reaction.

We all have our off days. Some people, like Jake, simply have a short fuse. Someone with a short fuse doesn't (in fact they often can't) stop to recognise the other emotions that are happening for them. They just leap straight to the end of the fuse and—boom!

When people ask me for help to manage their anger, they're really talking about poorly expressed anger, such as temper. I always ask them about their other emotions, and they very often tell me that they don't feel any other emotions—just the anger rising up within them. Often that's because somewhere in the past, usually in those vulnerable childhood years, they've learnt to bury their feelings as a way of managing emotional pain. It's no wonder they've developed a short fuse!

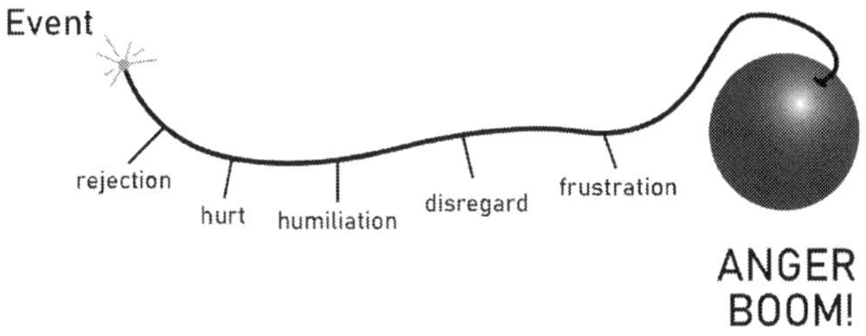

Once they get better at recognising the emotions that trigger their explosive anger, the fuse becomes longer. They have time to slow down and put out that fire before it's too late.

So experiencing healthy anger is really all about recognising intense emotions, acknowledging them, and learning to express them in calm and assertive ways. If we remember that anger in itself is not a bad thing —it's natural that people may behave in ways that are out of sync with our need for regard and respect and that we will have challenging emotions around that. Recognising that this is what's happening can be hugely empowering. It creates motivation to change. It reminds us to set boundaries so that we have healthier, more authentic, and respectful relationships. Sandra, for example, didn't see any problem in teasing Jake; she meant no harm. When he was able to let her know that he found it disrespectful, she was able to consider his point of view.

It's quite possible to get better at recognising and expressing anger in healthy, assertive ways. The place to start is by becoming master of our emotions so that they do not master us.

Emotions and Feelings: What's the Difference?

In everyday language, we tend to use the words 'emotions' and 'feelings' interchangeably. However, for the purpose of understanding the difference between poorly expressed anger and assertive anger, let's look at these terms from the following perspective: Emotions happen in the body. Feelings happen in the mind.

Emotions Happen in the Body

An emotion, as we've seen, is an actual physical experience. When we have an emotion, such as fear, anger, or excitement, we can sense it—it's a sudden surge of energy located somewhere in the body.

For example, when you're upset about something, you may notice that your heart pounds or your shoulders tense up, and when you're excited, your heart flutters and you feel a rush of joy in your chest.

Emotions happen as the result of a stimulus. For example, if someone was aggressive towards you (the stimulus), your body would naturally prepare itself for survival (the result). It would go into fight, flight or freeze mode and you would experience an emotion such as fear.

Feelings Happen in the Mind

Feelings, on the other hand, happen in the mind. They are more about the actual interpretation of an event, than a reaction to it.

So first, you experience the emotion in your body, e.g. fear, then you observe it with your mind, and decide what this means for you. Let's call it the *I'm observing that I'm feeling ...* part of ourselves.

If someone is aggressive towards you, for example, you feel the emotional reaction of fear in your system. Your mind then observes that and decides, 'I'm observing that I'm feeling frightened.' This consciously aware part of the mind is the part that makes rational choices and decisions. When we respond from this conscious part of ourselves, instead of letting emotions take charge, we get to observe the emotion, think about it, and decide what we want to do next. This means we can respond in an intentional way, rather than simply being triggered to retaliate.

Doesn't this just sound oh too easy! Feel the emotion. Decide what to do about it, and then have a wonderfully calm and adult response to any situation! The reality is that we can't always do this, because experiences, especially intense experiences, happen so quickly. Emotions flare up so fast, there's no time for the *I'm observing that I'm feeling* ... part of ourselves to reflect on the situation and make a calm decision. So, Boom!

But there is a way to overcome this. The trick is to get really good at noticing our emotions on an everyday basis. That way, we'll be able to access the *I'm observing that I'm feeling...* part of ourselves more easily when challenging circumstances come up.

Getting Better at Noticing Emotions

Some people are naturally good at tuning into their emotions; others, like Jake, find it more of a challenge. The question is: if apart from anger, you find it difficult to get in touch with your emotions, how do you learn to get better at it?

Actually, it's not that hard. There is a very effective and easy way to get much better at it. I've shared this method with many clients who've found it very useful in helping them get more in touch with their emotional self.

Quick Win

Start by noticing your physical sensations. Because emotions live in your body, they can be felt in your body. These sensations vary from person to person. You'll find that you have your own individual ones. To help you get an idea of how it works, some common ones are:

- Heart pounding
- Heaviness in your core
- Flutter in your chest
- Warmth in your heart
- Churning in the stomach
- Tension in the jaw
- Smile on your lips
- Tension in the shoulders

Here's what I suggested to Jake.

'Each day, when any noteworthy event happens—a negative event, or even a positive event—tune in and notice the sensations in your body. Notice when your heart pounds, your stomach churns, your shoulders tense up, etc. These sensations happen because an emotion is happening, so ask yourself: "What is this emotion that I am feeling in my body? Is it sadness? Is it joy? Is it hurt? Is it excitement? Can I identify it?"'

As Jake started doing this, his temper diminished because he was able to catch the emotion before it triggered reactive outbursts. I also suggested to Sandra that she ask Jake about his feelings from time to time, to help him get used to having that inner dialogue. In this way he was able to practise tuning into, and being familiar with, his emotions, rather than being controlled by them.

Once Jake got into the habit of this, he learnt to express himself to Sandra in more authentic, and thus effective, ways. In turn, Sandra was more able to understand how he was feeling.

Here's an example of their new, more assertive, way of expressing themselves.

Jake: 'I know you don't mean any harm when you tease me, but it makes me feel humiliated.'

Sandra: 'I'll do my best not to tease you. You know it's really just my sense of humour.'

Jake: 'It felt like you were asking me to fix the cupboard door because you thought I was too stupid to have noticed it.'

Sandra: 'No, that's not what I meant. I just remembered how busy you are, and I wanted to help by reminding you.'

Jake surprised himself by realising that he really didn't mind telling Sandra when he was feeling vulnerable. All these years, the scared and humiliated schoolboy within him had been doing battle, trying to protect him. Now that little boy within was able to let go, and the more adult Jake was able to step in and take control of his life. The authenticity of being able to say, 'I'm hurting, I'm worried, I'm feeling humiliated,' was a tremendous relief. And Sandra had only the greatest of respect for him when he opened his heart and spoke his true feelings.

To recognise that we feel emotions, such as humiliation or fear or rejection, and to express that to someone is one of the most authentic and courageous things we can do. It's the path to having much more confident and happier relationships. So if you sometimes struggle to express anger in these healthy ways, start by learning how to tune in to your emotions. That way they'll be less likely to suddenly appear and surprise you. For example, you can say to yourself, 'Oh yes, I recognise this feeling of humiliation,' and in doing so you step back a little. You can then use the *I'm observing that I'm feeling ...* part of your mind to decide how to respond to a situation.

For the handy **Anger Release Steps** worksheet, visit the free companion course at

www.howkindpeople.com

Anger, Depression, and Anxiety

Tamsin, 49

Tamsin came to me for help because she was feeling increasingly depressed and anxious. She was having problems at work. A habitual people-pleaser, Tamsin found it hard to say no to her colleagues' requests to share their workload with her, but later she'd feel resentful and criticise herself for being a doormat. She justified their behaviour by saying that they had too much to do, and she also reasoned that since she was quick at completing tasks, why not help them out. It seemed that she had a habit of taking on other people's responsibilities.

During our sessions, Tamsin told me about the teenage neighbour who had sexually abused her when she was eight years old. I noticed that Tamsin was quite blasé as she described this. She'd talked about it with a counsellor in her early twenties, and considered herself to be over it now. Tamsin had come to conclude that the boy probably had confidence issues as he was very overweight and unattractive. She thought that he was sexually experimenting because he had little chance of doing so with girls of his own age. She also wondered if he'd been abused himself.

Tamsin was a highly intelligent woman who had learnt to use her mind to manage this trauma. She described the incidents in terms of, ‘He couldn’t help it.’

Choosing to ‘intellectualise away’ these events was a much easier way for Tamsin to think about them than saying, ‘What he did to me was a terrible thing.’

Yet, something was niggling at me. I was curious about what Tamsin had done with the emotions from these events. As I mentioned earlier, our emotions don’t just disappear because we ignore them—they’re an energy which must be released in some form. As we worked together, Tamsin realised that she’d been suppressing a huge chunk of fear and anger towards this boy, and that squashing all this down had contributed greatly to her depression and anxiety. Once she expressed this clearly, she was able to openly admit that she had these feelings, to talk about them, and to release them.

It’s Not Unkind to Acknowledge Mistreatment

It’s not uncommon to form this habit of intellectualising away the traumas that have hurt us deeply. That’s partly because, like Tamsin, we find that it’s both psychologically and emotionally easier to bear if we can try to make sense of it. Also, not blaming or judging means we can remain in the role of the good and kind person, show empathy (though misplaced) and have compassion for our fellow human beings. So we end up saying things like

'She didn't mean it.'

'He didn't know any better.'

'It was their own upbringing: how could they know anything different?'

The confusion here is about responsibility. If a person has mistreated you in some way, that is *their responsibility*. Yes, you can offer kindness, understanding, and compassion, but their behaviour is their responsibility and it is perfectly OK for you to acknowledge that.

If you don't acknowledge that they are responsible for their own behaviour, you may just as well be saying to them, 'You're Ok, but I'm not OK'. It isn't being consciously kind, because you are devaluing your own worth, and you're not offering that person the opportunity to take responsibility for their life; consequently, they cannot learn and grow.

Sum Up Points

- Feeling angry is not a problem in itself—rather it's the way we express that anger that is the problem.
- Poorly expressed anger, such as temper, is the result of other emotions which trigger the reaction.
- The trick is to get good at noticing those other

emotions before that level of explosive anger is reached.

- Understanding the difference between feelings and emotions helps immensely in that process.
- Anger that is not expressed outwardly can cause depression and anxiety.
- People often intellectualise mistreatment from others as a way of managing the hurt.
- You can understand a person's behaviour from an intellectual point of view, *and* also be angry about it. You don't have to choose one or the other.

Self-Reflective Questions for How to Say 'I'm Angry'

What other emotions am I aware of that trigger angry outbursts?

How can I express anger in more appropriate ways?

What kind words can I say to soothe my inner child who is feeling the distressing emotions?

In your **Intentional Life Plan**, you will find the template: **Expressing Anger**. Consider these self-reflective questions and use your conclusions to help you complete it.

www.howkindpeople.com

Chapter 14
How to Say 'Enough!'

Carly, 47

When Carly was just five years old, her mother walked out of the family home, never to return. Unable to manage his pain and grief, Carly's father descended into long-term depression. As the years moved on, he became more and more irritable, and intolerant of Carly. He constantly found fault in everything she did, judging and criticising her every effort to gain his approval.

In adulthood, Carly had relationships with several men who were equally critical. She went on to marry someone with whom she endured ten years of disrespect and disparagement. But finally, Carly had had enough.

'Looking back, it seems odd that I put up with it for so long,' she told me, 'but I guess it was because it seemed normal to me; I'd never known any other kind of treatment from a man.'

Carly was wise to see the link between her relationship with her father and the other men in her life. It's very often the case that we're drawn to a person because they remind us of an important figure from our earliest years—often a parent or a caregiver. Whether that person was a kind and positive influence, or an abusive and negative one, it's the familiarity that attracts us. As we saw in Part 2 'Why We Find It So Hard to Be Assertive', the subconscious is extremely powerful in dictating our choices and decisions. On a conscious level, much of the time we have no clue that we're being drawn to a certain type of person. I've found though, that often, when people get so fed up with repeating the same challenging experiences, they begin to ask the question, 'Is there a pattern here?' It's then that they decide to have some therapy sessions to help break that pattern.

We're Spiritually Driven and Biologically Hardwired

Human beings are wisdom seekers. We're spiritually driven and biologically hardwired to seek out challenges, so that we can grow into our potential. This is why we're often subconsciously driven to try to figure out the issues of our childhood. One way we do this is by trying to correct the very same mistakes we saw our parents make—within our own adult relationships. These can be mistakes we witnessed them make with each other, or mistakes they made in their parenting of us.

For example, a child who grew up watching their parents in constant battle may grow up to be an adult who unconsciously seeks out aggressive partners so that they can finally restore peace. Or, a person whose parent had affairs may seek out partners who cheat, in an attempt to learn how to get them to be faithful.

If, like so many people, you too have had experiences in your childhood that left you feeling confused, traumatised, and unloved, you'll likely have been carrying a deep desire to resolve that. It's this desire that may well have (completely outside of your awareness) propelled you towards people who seemed somehow familiar.

And, like so many people, it's quite likely that you've tried to resolve those issues in ways that haven't worked—perhaps using misguided kindness by letting people off the hook, pleasing and placating, saying yes when you want to say no, and all those other non-assertive ways that simply keep people going around in circles. If this is you, remember it's very common—you're certainly not alone!

Emerging Patterns

There's a reason that many therapists ask their clients about their childhood. It's not just because they want to understand why their clients feel the way they do—it's also because it helps to uncover beliefs and patterns that may well be dictating their current relationships. And as clients describe the same issues occurring across several different relationships, therapists begin to help them see an emerging pattern.

Even though it can sometimes be a little confronting for a client to come to this awareness, it can also bring relief, because becoming self-aware brings possibility for change. They can begin to question whether it really is all these other people that have been causing their problems. Could it just be that they, themselves, have been thinking and behaving in ways that create—and reinforce—their issues?

This insight is priceless. Instead of wishing another person would change, they can take the responsibility, and the courage, to change themselves; they can begin to consider being intentional about their choice of relationships, and how they will behave within those relationships.

As Carly was able to take a step back and recognise the patterns that had been playing out in her life, she began to let go of the past and her constant need for approval. She began to provide love and acceptance for herself, and in doing so, she became less reliant on the approval of others. She met a new man and took the confidence and communication techniques she'd learnt into this new relationship.

'I'm loving that we have this easy relationship,' she told me. 'He doesn't criticise me, or make me feel unworthy. I think it's because I value myself, so he automatically values me too.'

It was a year later when Carly contacted me for further sessions. She was seeking help to sort out a troubling friendship. Mary, a long-term friend, would often disrespect Carly, putting her down, making cutting remarks and being generally negative about her successes in life. It was getting Carly down. 'I never really noticed just how bad it was before,' she told me.

It can be like this. Wisdom is an ongoing journey; life will always present us with challenges to help us grow and evolve a little more. As you become more assertive in one relationship, you may well notice problems in other relationships as you begin to see the contrast. Where previously Carly had let Mary's disrespect pass her by, now she was very clear that she deserved better.

Carly had an inkling of why her friend behaved in this way. In their teen years, Carly had been the popular and attractive one, while Mary had taken a few more years to catch up. Even though Mary was now a highly successful woman in her own right, it seemed to Carly that when it came to their friendship, she was still experiencing those old feelings of inadequacy and competitiveness from their teen years.

While Carly was able to intellectualise Mary's behaviour, her emotions were telling her that something had to change if their relationship was to survive. The problem was that Carly found it very difficult to speak up. She wanted to be able to say something *in the moment*, at the point that Mary insulted her, but every time it happened, Carly's mind would just go blank.

On reflection, Carly told me, she'd had this same struggle in other friendships. Someone would say something disrespectful, and instead of being able to speak up, she'd just totally freeze. Then later she would cogitate on it, and wish she'd said something.

Maybe you can relate to Carly. Somebody does or says something to upset you, you clam up, and then later you think, 'Why didn't I just say ... ?'

We all do this sometimes. As we saw in chapter 7 'When Emotions Hold Us Hostage', if you're aware that you're under threat in some way, or even if your subconscious thinks you are, the part of your brain that wants to help you (the amygdala) will place you into fight, flight or freeze mode so that you can cope better.

This is what was happening for Carly: the emotions caused by Mary's barbed comments—emotions such as hurt, anger, and humiliation—were creating a *stress response* which would then place Carly in freeze mode so her mind would go blank.

On reflection, Carly also recognised that when Mary made

those cutting remarks, it took her right back to when her father would criticise her—she'd felt so powerless then.

I taught Carly how to practise Emotional Freedom Techniques (EFT): a method to calm the amygdala and help let go of overwhelming emotions. She started a daily practice of EFT to help her let go of the anxiety that made her freeze up, and to let go of the powerlessness and hurt from the past. As she did this, she was more able to speak up and be her real self with Mary.

I've provided information and a video on learning how to use EFT to help release overwhelming emotions. You'll find them in your free companion course at:

www.howkindpeople.com

I highly recommend you watch this video. EFT is a very effective tool, which once learnt can be applied to any situation where you feel overwhelmed by any unwanted emotion. It can be used to help clear past traumas, deal with current fears, and also let go of worries about things that are coming up in the future.

The Power of US

Managing her overwhelming emotions was incredibly helpful for Carly. She also needed to think about what she wanted to say to Mary. She didn't want to be unkind, but she needed to find a way to communicate to Mary that her disrespect was unacceptable.

At first Carly looked for some quick phrases: some words she could rehearse so that when Mary made another nasty comment, she would be ready. She came up with:

'I feel so disrespected when you say that.'

'I don't know if you realise how much that hurts my feelings.'

This was a good strategy for dealing with Mary's *in the moment* comments, but the more Carly thought about it, the more she realised that she wanted to address their relationship as a whole.

Carly wanted to be more intentional about the relationship itself; she wanted to find a way to be authentic with Mary—to open her heart and let her know how worried she was about losing the friendship.

She decided the best way forward was to have an open and honest conversation. She was understandably nervous about making herself so vulnerable, especially as Mary was inclined to be so defensive.

To help her find courage, I suggested that Carly approach the conversation from the perspective of 'We and Us', rather than 'You and Me'.

Quick Win

I call this approach 'The Power of Us'. It's an extremely effective assertiveness technique. By focusing on the relationship itself, rather than on those in the relationship, any sense of judgement or criticism is removed from the conversation. It brings us back to being consciously kind, striving for the best outcome for everyone involved.

Carly thought about what she wanted to say to Mary. She jotted down a few notes and rehearsed her words. In our next session, Carly told me how her meeting with her friend went. She had invited Mary to go for a walk in a beautiful area they both knew well, and as they strolled along, Carly talked about their friendship and all the years they'd know each other. She shared how grateful she was for having had a good friend for such a long time. They reminisced about different stages in their childhood and growing up together. Carly focused on how she remembered that they'd been quite different at one stage in their teens, and how it had taken Mary a bit of time to blossom in her looks and personality, and how challenging that must have been for her.

By approaching the conversation from a focus on *us* and *our relationship*, Carly found it much easier to let Mary know that sometimes she felt like they were right back in those teen years. She said that at times she felt the competition was still there in the relationship because Mary could be so cutting. Those barbed comments hurt her feelings.

Mary hadn't been aware that she'd been doing this, nor had she been aware of the impact it was having on their friendship. Carly also brought a little humour into the conversation, saying that the next time either of them went into their child/teen selves again, they could tease each other about it. In having this deeply authentic and loving conversation, Carly and Mary became closer, and each, in her own way, took another step forward on their paths to wisdom.

Farah, 44 and Steve, 49

Farah and Steve had been married for twenty years. They were a likeable couple—people were drawn to their friendly nature and generous spirits. However, there were occasions, usually at family gatherings, when Steve would fly off the handle, often blaming Farah and other family members for some perceived disrespect. Everyone would feel embarrassed by his outburst.

Steve wasn't a bad person by any means. He was warm-hearted, loving, and caring; he often told Farah how much she meant to him and how he couldn't live without her. That, coupled with the fact that Steve was only triggered in certain situations, had made it easy for Farah to ignore the problem between his flare-ups.

This is a common pattern. When there is some issue that keeps popping up from time to time, it's so easy to forget about it in between times when the waters are calm. None of us like to be in a negative space, so we put it aside and hope it won't happen again.

Inevitably though, it does pop up again, and we try to deal with it by reacting in the moment. This quick fix approach, however, is a misguided way to try to manage it because it doesn't resolve the problem in the long term.

Farah knew that Steve's temper flare-ups stemmed from a deep-rooted insecurity. As a child, his parents had been extremely critical of him; he'd felt unloved and worthless. Now, whenever he thought he was being put down, he'd behave like a hurt and angry child. Family gatherings especially triggered him; on a subconscious level they took him right back to his childhood home environment.

Because Farah understood Steve's insecurities, she would try to smooth things over. When he lost his temper, she would say things like 'There's no need to get upset. It's OK,' which, she confided to me, never really helped.

Farah was right. It didn't help at all, because trying to smooth things over for the sake of peace and quiet had simply been reinforcing the message to Steve that having a temper tantrum was OK. When someone is reacting from a state of insecurity, it seems like the most logical thing to do is try to reassure and pacify them. However, temper tantrum behaviour is unacceptable—they need to know that.

Farah had had enough. She wanted to find a more effective way to respond to the situation. I suggested that a more consciously kind approach would be to focus not only on Steve's need for understanding and compassion, but also to consider her own and others' right for respect.

Instead of waiting until Steve was having a tantrum and then trying to calm him in the moment, I proposed she find ways to bolster his confidence in times of calm, then be more assertive when he was behaving inappropriately. Farah found ways to boost Steve's confidence in their day-to-day life by complimenting his achievements and showing her appreciation of him. She also came up with the following phrases to use when Steve was behaving unfavourably.

'Your behaviour is inappropriate and disrespectful.'

'You are embarrassing yourself right now.'

'If you stop now, you'll catch it before it's too late.'

It wasn't easy to make this change—Farah had gotten so much into the pattern of trying to fend off Steve's temper. However, she took the courage to be more authentic and make changes in the way she responded to Steve's outbursts. It took a few attempts, but in time Steve became much calmer and more adult in the way he handled situations that he perceived to be challenging. The two things that really helped Farah were:

She made a big effort to bolster Steve in times of calm so that he felt more confident within himself.

She had her prepared assertive phrases ready to state when Steve lost his temper.

When It's Time to Say Goodbye

We've seen that Carly's way of saying 'Enough!' was a combination of working on her own overwhelming emotions and having an authentic conversation with her friend. The relationship was not only saved—it blossomed.

Farah was able to let Steve know that she had had enough of his disrespectful outbursts, and she helped him find better ways of handling his challenges.

However, sometimes reaching the point of 'Enough!' means recognising that a relationship is never going to work. It could be that someone has been disregarding us for some time, maybe even since the beginning of the relationship. It can happen that as we grow in confidence, we step back a little and see that disrespect has always been there, and maybe we have always misguidedly let it go because we didn't want to seem unkind, or to be rejected.

If a relationship is fraught, it can take a while to recognise that it isn't ever going to work. What tends to happen is that we get so caught up in trying to fix the problem that we can't see the relationship for what it truly is. So much focus is put on wondering, 'Why is this person behaving this way? What have I said or done? Why do they not hear me? Why do they promise to change but then they don't?' All this can take up such a huge amount of mental and emotional energy that we just can't see the wood for the trees.

Because we are solution-focused beings, we can get very much caught up in trying to solve a relationship. Especially if it is a replay of a childhood relationship that we're still trying to resolve. Instead of putting so much focus on trying to figure out things, and then find solutions, it can sometimes be much more helpful to consider these questions:

'Is this person in the right emotional space to be my good friend, my good partner, my good spouse?'

'Are they at a different place on the path towards life's wisdom?

'Is it fair to expect them to share the same goals as mine if they just can't do that?'

Asking yourself these types of questions can bring huge relief. In recognising that a person is simply being *who they are* and that *they are where they're at on their journey*, you can begin to disentangle yourself from the confusion you are experiencing.

Creating Space for the Most Important Relationship

Sometimes being assertive is just as much about how we treat ourselves, as it is about our relationships with others. Saying 'Enough!' then, can be about having a deeply authentic conversation with yourself, asking, 'How much more of my precious life do I want to spend in this energy space, with this person, in this situation?' It can take huge courage to admit that you may have to give up on a relationship, knowing that you'll have to experience that loss in order to move forward. That can be so hard. I know. But letting go of the need to keep trying to fix it means that you get to create the space and time to focus on the most important relationship of all—the one you have with yourself.

It's when we get good at *that* relationship that we tend to attract people who will love us equally. I've seen this happen time and time again, with clients, with friends, and in my own experience.

Saying goodbye to a relationship doesn't necessarily have to be a big wrench. Sometimes relationships work well in certain chapters of our lives, but then they no longer serve us as we grow and mature into a different version of ourselves. We may have moved a little further along the path of wisdom and left that person behind, or they may have left us behind. But this isn't to say that the connection we had with them wasn't worth it at the time. You may come back around to the relationship when each of you has had time and space to reflect and grow. Or you may consign that relationship to the past, knowing that it was applicable to your life at the time.

And if you do decide that it is time to say goodbye to a challenging relationship, it's important to know that nothing in this life is ever wasted. We can look at the good experiences and have an appreciation for them, and we can also look at the more challenging experiences and ask, 'What have I learnt from having this experience?'

That's when wisdom arrives in our hearts.

Sum Up Points

- We often subconsciously seek out people who remind us of the caregivers in our childhood.
- We are driven to learn, grow, and evolve.
- We seek out relationships where we can try to resolve the mistakes we witnessed in our parents' relationships, or the mistakes they made in their parenting of us.

- Stopping to reflect, and recognising unhelpful patterns is a huge turning point; it's an opportunity to begin a process of change.
- When we learn to be more assertive, we can resolve those issues in our current relationships.
- As we become more assertive, we notice, by contrast, other areas of life and relationships that may need work.
- You can find the courage to be authentic and to challenge relationship problems by using 'We and Us', rather than 'You and Me'.
- Be careful not to get so caught up in trying to fix a relationship that you miss the fact that the person simply isn't able to give you what you need.
- Sometimes 'Enough!' means ending a relationship, but nothing is ever wasted. Wisdom comes from asking, 'What can I learn from that experience?'

Self-Reflective Questions for How to Say 'Enough!'

1. What are the most important relationships in my life?
2. How is my being responsible *to* these people different from being responsible *for* them?
3. What We and Us statements can I use for better communication?

4. What have I learnt from challenging relationships that I can do differently next time?

In your **Intentional Life Plan**, you will find the template: **Saying 'Enough!'** Consider these self-reflective questions and use your conclusions to help you complete it.

www.howkindpeople.com

Part Six

How Kind People Get Great Relationships

Have you ever heard the saying 'You are the average of the people you spend the most time with?'

It can be quite a revelation to come to this understanding, and actually very helpful. It means we can begin to be more intentional about which people we choose to have in our lives—or at least about how much time we choose to spend with some of them.

A lot of us haven't been taught to intentionally *choose* the types of people we have in our lives. We just drift into connections with people without giving it much thought because no one has ever suggested that we could A) consider our self-worth and B) select the types of people who can enhance that.

If we hold certain self-limiting beliefs, such as *I'm not good enough* or *I don't deserve to be valued*, it can lead to choosing the wrong people—people who don't know how to respect us.

Also, tied in with these unhelpful beliefs, as I've mentioned, there may be an inner drive to choose people to help us try and figure out problems from past relationships.

Because of all this we can end up feeling confused, wondering where we stand, questioning whether we should assert ourselves more, or if we are just being overly sensitive. This confusion is so common. I've seen it many times in my therapy room, I've seen it in my own relationships, and I can guess it may resonate for you too?

In the following section of the book, we're going to be addressing this.

Chapter 15
How to Know Where You Stand

Bill, 36 and Tania, 31

Bill and Tania came to see me for couples therapy. They had been together for two years. Bill lived with Tania and her two daughters Chloe, fourteen and Charlotte, nine.

In the beginning, their relationship had been wonderful, but much of the past year had been fraught with rows and upset. The main issue for Tania was the amount of time Bill spent with his ex-wife Veronica.

Bill and Veronica had parted company a few years previously after a fourteen-year marriage. They'd been very young when they married and had their son Nathan. It had been a happy marriage, but in time they'd simply changed as people and grown apart.

When they decided to divorce, there was no acrimony. Nathan remained with his mother and she and Bill remained good friends.

Bill would often drop by the house to spend time with Nathan, and Veronica would cook him a meal—just like the old days.

Tania said, 'It's not like I really think there's something going on between them—it's just that the whole set-up is so intimate. He just pops around as if he still lives there. It feels like a betrayal of our life together. Sometimes I find out he's lied about it, because he's trying to avoid a row, but then that makes me feel all the more insecure.'

Clearly, it was better that Bill and Veronica got on well for the sake of their son. However, popping in for dinner and playing 'happy families' was disrespectful to his new relationship.

When I asked if Tania had understood this arrangement when she first met Bill, she told me that she hadn't wanted to come across as needy. 'I don't think I realised how close they still were, or that Bill expected to carry on like this,' she said. Clearly the parameters of the relationships had never been discussed in detail.

There are no rules for how people should navigate their relationships with ex-partners and blended families; it comes down to personal choice. What is important, though, is that everyone knows where they stand—and often people don't. It's a common problem in a world where people do their best to get along after a breakup, especially where children are concerned. As I remind my couples clients, even if they break up, they'll always have a relationship of some sort, if they have had children together; it's just that it will be a different type of relationship—one that needs to be defined.

I asked Bill how he saw the situation. He told me that he felt completely stressed out by all the upsets, and caught in the middle. He didn't want to turn his back on Veronica—they were good friends and he felt guilty to a degree about not being there so much for Nathan. However, he loved Tania and wanted to make their relationship work.

Bill was making the classic mistake of trying to keep everyone happy. When we do this, we invariably keep no one happy. No one knows where they stand and everyone feels that little bit insecure because there is no real clarity or true authenticity.

It's important to note that trying to keep everyone happy is not the same thing as seeking a win-win outcome. When we seek a win-win outcome, the emphasis is on *outcome.* We are considering the bigger picture of a situation. Everyone has equal measure of regard. It's often about compromise and sitting with discomfort, while changes take place and new norms are created.

Keeping everyone happy, however, is a different kettle of fish. It tends to be reactive and based on quick fixes. People hop from one person to the other, pleasing each in the current moment.

Tania didn't know where she stood in her relationship with

Bill. Despite his protestations that he loved her, his actions appeared to be to the contrary. Bill was distressed and exhausted trying to keep his past and present relationships on an equal footing. The children were all caught up in the mix.

There had been no boundaries, until Tania, sick of not knowing where she stood, became more assertive. She had requested to come for couples therapy and Bill had agreed. That was their first step. Now they needed to be more intentional about how they were going to navigate their relationships so that they could find a win-win outcome for everyone.

Boundaries were needed.

Bill wanted to keep his good friendship with Veronica and also wanted to spend as much time with Nathan as possible. However, he could see that from Tania's point of view, casually popping in for dinner at the old family home was not appropriate or respectful to his new relationship.

The solution was to come up with some boundaries that would ensure that everyone's feelings and needs were considered. They agreed on specific days and times when Bill would spend time with his son. He had a discussion with Veronica about the new boundaries of their relationship, explaining that he would not be coming around for impromptu dinners at the house, but—if everyone agreed—they could all meet together at a restaurant for special occasions, such as

Nathan's birthdays.

He also spoke from the heart to Tania. He made it clear that he still had great affection for Veronica and that this would not change. Though somewhat confronting for Tania, his authenticity helped make a shift for her, because now everything was out in the open. She now had the truth and could stop worrying about where she stood, plus he was also making the effort to set some respectful guidelines about his former relationship.

These changes were challenging for all of them: Tania had to find the courage to speak her truth and ask Bill to come to therapy. Bill had to let go of his habit of casually popping in at the old family home and he had to acknowledge that his relationship with Veronica would need to be different in the future. Veronica had to respect that he was in a new relationship and that their friendship would be more formal. However, by setting these boundaries, they were all able to find a win-win outcome and move forward to happier, more peaceful times where everyone knew where they stood.

You are Far More Powerful than You Realise

The situation with Bill, Tania, and Veronica could have gone on for years, causing increasing distress and bad feeling. Many couples get caught up in this gap between past and current relationships with no one really knowing where they stand.

Tania, however, decided to step up and take responsibility for her own happiness instead of constantly blaming Bill and Veronica.

Most people, as we know, have kindness in their hearts; they haven't meant to commit the great crime that we're mentally accusing them of. The worst they could be accused of is lacking awareness. As was Bill's case.

Yet, when we view them as being purposely disrespectful, we hand over all our power to them. Assertiveness is about understanding that *we* are responsible for where we stand in our relationships—that we make our own choices. In seeking couples therapy, Tania was stepping into her own power.

The fact is that unless someone has literally physically forced you into a situation, it is you, yourself that has placed yourself there. This can be hard to acknowledge, because we're all so quick to judge and make other people responsible for our own happiness.

Certainly, other people can *trigger* our feelings, but learning to be more assertive is all about owning those feelings and choosing what to do about that. There can be something very comforting in knowing that we can take responsibility for our own happiness. Once we stop blaming others, and begin to acknowledge that responsibility, we can become empowered again because we're taking ownership of our own life. It means we choose where we stand in our relationships, instead of trying to guess.

Deciding What Matters to You

Kim, 24

Kim had spent a great deal of time focusing on her studies and building her career in medicine. Consequently, she hadn't had much experience socialising or dating. Now she wanted to get out there, have some fun, and 'Maybe I could even meet Mr Right,' she said, smiling at me shyly.

Kim didn't have any trouble meeting men. She had a profile on a dating website and a friend had set her up on dates too.

The trouble was that Kim had no idea about how she should behave, or what she should expect from these men. If she didn't like them, she'd feel guilty about hurting their feelings by saying no to a second date. If something felt *off* on a date, she'd wonder if she was being over-cautious or if she should trust her instincts.

On other occasions, if she really liked someone, her emotions would overwhelm her, and she'd get all tongue-tied when trying to make conversation.

'It feels like a minefield!' she told me.

Then there were the rules: should she be the one to suggest

meeting up again? Who should pay the bill? Was she expected to kiss on the first date? When should they sleep together? Kim was very confused—she had no idea where she stood with these men. Consequently, her supposed fun time dating was turning into an anxious nightmare.

When I asked Kim what she herself actually wanted from these dates, she looked at me blankly. She had no real idea beyond that they treat her with respect.

'But what does that actually look like?' I prompted. 'Can you be more specific?'

Kim had never stopped to consider what respect meant for her personally. And that's not at all unusual. People often say that they want regard and respect from others, but they haven't thought about what that specifically means to them.

Because of her lack of experience, Kim had the idea that there were rules of dating which all her peers knew about—something she'd missed out on because she'd been so busy with her studies.

I encouraged her to instead start thinking about what was important to her personally, and to create her own **Intentional Life Plan**.

Sometimes people get confused about setting boundaries because they have the idea that there are some *rules set in stone* which they must adhere to. In truth, it's much more about making those guidelines personal to you. That's why I've included the **Intentional Life Plan** for you as part of this book. It's your life and what you choose to expect from others is your entitlement. For example, if you want someone to dress well when going out with you, then that is your choice. If you don't mind if someone turns up in scruffy old jeans and a t-shirt, then that is your choice too.

People confuse being assertive with persuading someone to adhere to their own wishes and values. That can feel like a power struggle, but whenever there is an imbalance of power—that's not really assertiveness. It's not your place to force someone to toe the line of your outlook on life.

Real assertiveness is about you being very clear on your own boundaries and then making that clear to others. They can then decide if they're happy with that. If not, they'll move on, and this will make room in your life for someone who is more of a match.

The first step then, is in deciding what matters to you. This is being truly assertive. It's about saying, 'These are my values. This is the real authentic me, no games, no time-wasting. I respect you enough to make myself clear because I am OK, and you are OK too.' It is a consciously kind way of being because it's about looking at the bigger picture of your life, thinking it through and being intentional, rather than reacting to in-the-moment events and trying to force someone to bow to your wishes.

In our session, I helped Kim explore a range of different scenarios so that she could mull over how she felt and what she wanted. She started by thinking about what she didn't want. This helped her come up with a useful list of what she did want.

She decided that:

- If a man turned up late for their first date, she would let it go. However, she would make it clear that timekeeping was important to her. If he did it the next time, she wouldn't see him again.
- She wouldn't kiss until the second date.
- She wouldn't sleep with a man until the fourth date at least, and then only if she felt very comfortable.
- She wouldn't respond to someone who called her after 10pm.
- If someone didn't respond to a message, she would send one more, then stop.
- She would always split the bill.
- She would listen to how a man spoke about his friends and family to help her gauge whether he was a respectful type of person.
- She would ask him about his future plans, to assess if he was a committed type of person.

Another thing Kim worried about was how to end a date.

Should she be the one to suggest meeting again? She felt too shy to do that, but then again, she didn't want to give the impression that she wasn't interested. She settled on this phrase which she could rehearse and have ready to say: 'I had a great time. (pause) Let me know if you would like to meet up again.'

Having these guidelines in place was a huge help for Kim because it meant she didn't have to worry, or think on the spot, when emotions took over. She included these guidelines in her **Intentional Life Plan** so that she had something she could always refer to. She told me: 'It's like asking a mentor for advice.'

First, Be Clear on Where You Stand with Yourself

There are no right or wrong answers to what you should expect from others. We all have our own values and different standards about various aspects of life. It's a very personal decision and may well change over time as your life changes and you grow in confidence.

Knowing where you stand is far less about where you stand with others, than it is being clear on where you stand with yourself. Once you know that, being assertive is simply a matter of communicating it in the most respectful, consciously kind way you can.

Becoming more confident is an ongoing process. There will always be niggles, challenges, and opportunities to learn and grow. There is no perfect friend, spouse, or family member. We all have faults. It's about deciding which faults you can live with.

If you're lucky, the special people in your life will take the same attitude towards you!

Sum Up Points

- We need to take responsibility for our own happiness by being clear with others.
- Be honest with yourself about how you feel. It's OK to feel your feelings whether they are justified by others or not.
- If you tell someone you don't like their behaviour, make sure you explain why: the meaning you attach to it and the feelings that you experience.
- Real assertiveness is about being very clear on our own guidelines and then making them clear to others.
- What you want is personal to you.
- Knowing where you stand is far less about where you stand with others, than it is being clear on where you stand with yourself.

Self-Reflective Questions for How to Know Where You Stand

- Who is responsible for my happiness?
- Which life area needs most attention from me right now?
- Am I clear on my personal guidelines: for example, how I want to speak to myself and treat myself?

In your **Intentional Life Plan**, you will find the template: **Knowing Where You Stand**. Consider these self-reflective questions and use your conclusions to help you complete it.

www.howkindpeople.com

Chapter 16

How to Stop Rescuing and Start Supporting

David, 45

David came for help with his confidence. As we worked together, I was pleased to see that he was making good progress, but there was one issue we kept coming back round to—the relationship between his wife and their twenty-three-year-old son Greg. They didn't get along, and David was stuck in the middle.

There was a pattern. David would have lunch with Greg, who would tell him all about his issues with Mum. Then his wife would lie next to him in bed at night and tell him all her woes and concerns about Greg.

It upset David greatly to see his wife and son constantly at loggerheads. He was always trying to pull them together—suggesting ways they communicate with each other, and things they could do to make it better. The constant hypervigilance was causing David so much anxiety. 'I'm beginning to feel really fed up with the two of them!' he told me.

I could see how hard it was for David to be stuck in the middle, but I wondered why he felt so responsible for their relationship. I asked him to draw a diagram on the whiteboard to represent the family members and where they stood in relation to each other. He drew an image of himself stuck firmly in between his wife and son. This visual representation was powerful in helping David see how he was choosing to position himself. Even though he could see this so clearly, the belief that he had to be the one to make it all better was deeply embedded; it made it hard for him to imagine supporting his family from the sidelines.

Next, I asked David to list on the whiteboard all the things he feared for his family.

He wrote:

They'll eventually stop speaking to each other completely.

The family will fall apart.

They'll be unhappy.

I'll be unhappy.

I can't bear their pain—it feels like my pain.

As David stepped back and looked at the whiteboard, he had

a lightbulb moment. He realised that what he'd just written was describing his own childhood. It was his child self who was carrying this fear of the family falling apart.

David had grown up in a family where rows and aggression were part of daily life. He'd been constantly worried that something terrible was going to happen. As far back as he could remember, he was the one who tried to keep the peace, begging his parents to stop shouting at each other. He recalled when he was about eight years old, handing his pocket money back to his father, and saying, 'Use it to take Mummy to the pictures so you can make friends again.'

It was heart-breaking that little David had been so terrified that his family would fall apart. As we saw in chapter 4 'Rejection from the Tribe', on a deeply primal and subconscious level, we human beings believe that we must be part of a tribe to keep ourselves safe, and as children, we can experience this sense of insecurity in an especially intense way. So little David, desperate to keep his family together, took on the role of feeling worried and responsible about family relationships from very early on in his life.

Stepping Out of the Ring

Adult David began to see that he was playing much more of a part in his wife's and son's issues than he'd previously been aware of. His misguided way of trying to help them was a reaction to his own past—not a solution to their current situation.

'Oh,' he said. 'It's not just about those two. I see now, it's about us three!'

He now understood that his need to fix came from a sort of misplaced empathy. He couldn't bear to see his wife and son in pain because he remembered just how bad it had felt. He also had a deeply subconscious need to continue trying to repair his parents' relationship by re-enacting the role of rescuer.

It was a relief to realise this. Now he could see that by looking at the broader picture and being more intentional—rather than just rushing in to fix everything—he might be able to find the path to peace. I suggested that, instead of trying to fix his wife and son's relationship, he simply communicate his fears to them.

Sharing vulnerability was not a familiar way of being for David. It took courage to bear his soul and let them know the depth of his distress.

He sat his wife and son down and told them the things that he'd written on the whiteboard. He told them that he worried that they would continue to fall out and that one day they would drift apart completely. He told them how stressed he'd been and how sad it made him to see them unhappy.

David then set a clear boundary, stating that he would no

longer engage in conversation with either of them about their woes with the other. He didn't want to be stuck in the middle anymore. He reminded them how much he loved them, and he reassured them that he had every faith in them taking responsibility for their own relationship.

Things were a little uncomfortable at first, he told me; there were a lot of silences and glares. But after a couple of weeks, peace began to reign in the family. Now instead of constant anger and power struggles, there was an energy of calm and balance. Everybody benefited; it was a win-win-win situation!

Handing Back the Responsibility

It's always difficult to stand back and watch the people we love being unhappy, but if we keep jumping in to rescue them, are we being truly kind?

Rushing in to smooth things over doesn't ever fully resolve an issue—it will simply come back round again. So, rather than trying to smooth things over, it can be the kinder option to set some boundaries and hand people back their own responsibility. It can take courage to be assertive in this way. It may mean having to sit with discomfort for a short time while they take all this on board and sort themselves out; but ultimately this type of consciously thought-out kindness will give them the opportunity to learn and grow, as is their right to do in this life.

Ava, 67

Ava sought out my help because she was suffering from severe anxiety. Anxiety is often the body's way of saying to us: 'You've got too much stress in your life—it's time to do something about it!'

The stress may be linked to our day-to-day life, or even events from the distant past that haven't been resolved. Often, it's a combination of past and present.

I taught Ava some anxiety reduction techniques, such as ways to regain control of her runaway thoughts and EFT to manage her overwhelming panic. We also explored what was going on in her life that could be contributing to her stress.

Ava was very concerned about her relationship with her daughter Gill. Gill, a single mum of twins, was always struggling and short of funds. She was in the habit of asking Ava for money, and Ava was in the habit of giving it to her. Ava was retired and living on a very small pension; she really couldn't afford to keep bailing her daughter out.

In fact, Ava was even coming for her sessions infrequently because she lacked the funds to pay for regular sessions. I was tempted to give her a discount because I very much wanted her to get the benefit of regular sessions. However, I had to be very intentional and stand firm with Ava, so that she in turn would be encouraged to stand firm with Gill.

There was a pattern. Whenever Gill borrowed money from Ava, she would promise to pay the money back in instalments. Sometimes she would pay some of it back, but then the payments would stop. She never repaid the full amount, and Ava just didn't feel able to ask her for it.

I was curious. I asked her why not. Ava explained that she'd made mistakes when Gill was growing up. She didn't feel she'd been a good enough mother, and she felt so guilty about that. Now she felt that it was her responsibility to try to make it up to Gill.

Of course, there's nothing wrong with helping out family members, and to a certain extent, no matter what their age, our kids will always be 'our kids'. That's just human nature. But there comes a time when we must set some limits. Ava needed to stop rescuing Gill and find ways to support her instead.

Are You Supporting or Rescuing?

When we care about someone, we want to make sure they're secure and happy: of course! The problem is that we can get muddled up between supporting someone and rescuing them.

To support someone means empowering them to help themselves. It also means taking into consideration our own needs as well as theirs.

On the other hand, rescuing someone means rushing in and fixing things for that person, regardless of our own needs. This is often when things can get out of control—we can end up feeling overwhelmed by their demands.

By pretending that everything was OK, whilst quietly worrying, Ava wasn't being authentic with Gill. And because she was so consumed with guilt from Gill's childhood, she wasn't now giving Gill the opportunity to mature and reach her potential.

Ava realised that bailing Gill out all the time wasn't ever going to be a real solution; she needed to encourage Gill to take responsibility for herself. Hard as it might be, it was time to find courage and speak her truth.

Ava wanted to be more intentional about how she would manage things the next time Gill asked her for money. The problem was that she'd been down that road before. She'd often told Gill that this was the last time she would lend her money, and that she needed to be paid back. Gill would seem to understand and agree, but then nothing would change. I wondered how I could help Ava come up with some boundaries that would be clear for Gill.

Action-Oriented People

In chapter 10 'How to be Heard', we looked at how speaking

to people in their own language can make a huge difference in being heard by them. For example, if we can identify that they are visual, auditory or kinaesthetic, we can then match our own language style to theirs—*I see, I hear you, I feel* and so on.

Alongside language styles, it's also interesting to consider how we operate in the world. We experience this life through thinking, feeling, and taking action. Most of us have strengths in one or two of these areas. Those who are great at managing their emotions and mastering their thoughts may be weaker in taking action. Those who are good at monitoring their thoughts and taking action may not be so strong in managing and understanding emotions.

It's worth noting that if you keep telling someone how you feel and what you think, but nothing ever changes, it could well be that they're more action-oriented. They need to see something actually happening in order to understand the importance of it. Action-oriented people don't tend to pick up on very general concepts nor is it helpful to paint a picture for them. They also find it hard to grasp when, for example, you describe how you feel about an issue, because that doesn't give them any clue as to what needs to be done to fix the problem.

Ava saw that Gill was, indeed, an action-oriented person, and that she needed to use actions to make her point clearer to Gill. She came up with a plan.

A week or so later, Gill asked her for more money. Ava gave it to her and told her that there would be no more after that. She assuaged her feelings of guilt by reminding Gill that if she was ever desperate, she could always stay with her—that there would always be a roof for her— but no more money would be forthcoming.

Things were fine for a few weeks, until Gill ran out of money again, and again asked Ava to bail her out. But this time Ava said no.

At first, there were a few uncomfortable phone calls. In time though, Gill stopped asking Ava for money, as she came to terms with taking more responsibility for her own finances. Ava also took action by helping Gill make an appointment with a money-management advice centre, and she accompanied her to the meeting.

I had so much admiration for Ava for taking the courage to be assertive with her daughter. Gill wasn't a bad person; she just had no confidence with money, and the mixed messages she'd been getting from Ava had simply made it easier for her to carry on asking to be rescued.

In a relatively short time, mother and daughter became happier. Their relationship grew closer, as Ava let go of past guilt, and Gill became more of an adult friend to Ava, rather than remaining a needy child.

It can be remarkable how rapidly things can shift when we are a little more intentional about how we approach the difficulties in our relationships. Do remember, though, that learning to be more assertive is like building a muscle. You may well need to make a few attempts at your new way of being before you see the results you want. Keep going. Every time you take the courage to be the authentic you, you'll grow a little more confident. Practice makes permanent!

The Habitual Rescuer

Our two case studies: David and his family, and Ava and her daughter, are examples of how getting caught up in rescuing can impact specific relationships.

For some people however, rescuing is a lifelong habit that impacts everyone they meet.

Ruth, 54

Ruth gave me a huge beaming smile when she arrived for her first session. As we walked along the hallway towards the therapy room, she said, 'You know, if you mix flour, salt, and vinegar you can make a paste that will take the tarnish right off that front door handle.'

Momentarily, I was taken aback—and somewhat affronted. Then I took stock and observed what had just happened.

Noticing the reaction Ruth had brought up in me gave me a clue as to what she was probably bringing up in others. It seemed that Ruth was driven to please—to make herself helpful and likeable from the very start.

In our sessions, I saw that this was the case for many of her relationships. She described her struggles with her friends, and her confusion about why they would often push her away.

Ruth was so desperate to be liked that she would jump at the chance to help people. Whenever anyone had a problem, she'd be there. However, her desire to prove how kind and helpful she was meant that she never took the time to stop and ask anyone if they actually *wanted* her help. When people behave like this, it can come across as controlling and quite frankly rude!

Poor Ruth. I could see the familiar pattern of the habitual rescuer. The more she tried to please people, the more people rebuffed her, the more rejected she felt, and so the more the need to please people was reinforced. It was a never-ending cycle.

It is a sad fact that habitual rescuers can often struggle to hold onto relationships—of all types. They have no awareness that their input, uninvited, is coming across as pushy and arrogant. They alienate people, then wonder why they are being shunned.

In our sessions I gently helped Ruth to:

- Understand why, and how, her need to please had first come about
- Put herself in the shoes of the person being 'helped' to see the situation from their perspective
- To find more effective and consciously thought-out ways to communicate her kindness and offers of help

Ruth began to understand that much of her need to please was being driven by a deep-rooted fear of not being good enough—a message she had been repeatedly given in her past.

Habitual rescuing always comes from a place of fear. It's the little child within who has at some stage learnt that they must prove themselves extra worthy in order to get love, and to feel safe in the world. If you know someone like this, cut them a little slack—they really do mean well.

It's a useful distinction to understand that rescuing often comes from fear, where supporting comes from love.

Rescuing = Child-Based Reaction = Fear = Misplaced Kindness

It involves misguided empathy, fear of rejection, limiting beliefs, and overwhelming emotions.

Supporting = Adult Response = Love = Conscious Kindness

It involves healthy empathy, feeling connected and secure, helpful beliefs, and managed emotions.

Don't Assume

We all want to be kind, but when we focus on our own desire to please, we're actually thinking more about our own needs than what the other person actually wants. It's topsy-turvy because a lot of the time we don't realise this is what is happening; we think we're being pleasant and helpful!

I helped Ruth to see that she was assuming that people wanted her help and advice. Instead of focusing on her own need to prove how helpful she was, I recommended that she put those people centre stage, and first *ask them* if they wanted her help. As Ruth started approaching her relationships from this new perspective, she found that people warmed to her; they actually wanted her input and support!

Here are some examples of asking:

'I have an idea that could help you—do you want me to tell you?'

'I know someone who sells those—do you want their contact details?'

'I had that same experience and I learnt something from it—do you want me to share it with you?'

If you have a tendency to rush in and help, try this approach of asking first. Even if this feels a little wooden at first, do it anyway. You'll see that once you make the shift from focusing on your own need to please to focusing on the other person, it becomes far more authentic. It's real, they'll feel more valued and respected. And, curiously, you may just find that they'll be more open to your ideas!

There are of course times when someone truly does need to be rescued, but in most cases, the more consciously kind thing we can do is offer them support by being by their side, encouraging them, helping them to help themselves. Not only does this let them know that we have faith in their ability, it also sets clear boundaries about where we, and they, stand.

Remember too, that life is all about learning through our challenges. It's truly a kind act to encourage another person to learn their own lessons for themselves, rather than taking away that opportunity by rushing in and doing it all for them.

Four Great Ways to Support Someone

1. Listen to their worries, without trying to fix it for them

One of the kindest things we can do for someone is to just listen to them. Quite often people need to offload their worries; they feel much better simply by doing that. If you rush in and 'fix it' for them, you're denying them the opportunity to learn something.

2. Ask them supportive questions

This takes a little practice. Try focusing on what you would want to be asked in a difficult situation. These would be open questions, such as 'I wonder if there's a way round that? What can you do to make that better, or easier, or different?'

These types of questions will help a person feel truly supported, and able to think for themselves.

3. Offer them lots of validation and encouragement

'You're doing well.'

'I'm so impressed by how you did that.'

'You're an inspiration!'

These types of statements put you into the supportive role immediately, because they focus on the other person—not on you doing it for them.

Remember that by encouraging someone to help themselves, you're helping them to feel confident about managing not only the current issue, but their future challenges too!

4. Take time

It's so easy to rush in to help someone because it seems to save time. But a little patience now will pay dividends in time in the future as this person learns to be more independent of you.

Sum Up Points

- Sometimes we want to rescue other people's relationships because we want to solve poor relationships witnessed in our childhood.
- People are responsible for their own relationships.
- Rescuing people is always driven by misplaced empathy.
- We have a responsibility *to* others to be consciously kind—we are not responsible *for* them.
- Sometimes we have to sit with other people's discomfort while they work through their challenges.
- Sometimes we have to sit with our own discomfort too.
- The need to rescue can sometimes be driven by guilt.
- Rescuing people only reinforces their

powerlessness.

- Habitual rescuers are reacting from fear.
- You can break the rescue habit by asking people if they want help before you give it.

Self-Reflective Questions for How to Stop Rescuing and Start Supporting

1. Is there someone in my life who I tend to rescue rather than support?
2. What emotions come up for me if I see them having challenges?
3. What is the difference between me supporting this person and me rescuing them?

In your **Intentional Life Plan**, you will find the template: **Breaking the Rescue Habit**. Consider these self-reflective questions and use your conclusions to help you complete it.

www.howkindpeople.com

Chapter 17
How to Attract the Right People into Your Life

Heather, 37

As Heather came in for her first session, I noticed how pale and depressed she looked. She told me that she'd recently split up with her partner.

'It's the same pattern with every woman I meet,' she said. "At first they seem so polite and attentive. Then after a few months they start taking me for granted and treating me like dirt.'

I asked Heather what she did when this happened.

'Nothing really,' she said. 'I never want to come across as one of those whiny girlfriends.'

This fear of being whiny started with Heather's first girlfriend when she was just sixteen. She had cheated on Heather, and when Heather got upset, she'd called her mad and needy.

They'd all been so young and immature, but her accusations had stuck with Heather all these years.

I've met a lot of people who put up with disrespect because they worry about coming across as needy. It tends to happen because people are unsure of themselves and where they stand in relationships. It's so much easier to be assertive if you feel secure in your own sense of worth, and you know exactly what you want from a relationship.

I wondered whether Heather knew what *she* truly wanted from a relationship, and how much time she was putting into getting to know these women before getting romantically involved. She admitted that she tended to rush into relationships. She hated being alone; as soon as one relationship ended, she'd be straight out clubbing with her friends to find another. On reflection, Heather realised she hadn't been single for more than three months since her teens.

These disrespectful women in Heather's life were not bad people. They weren't going out of their way to put her down—they just hadn't reached a stage of maturity where they'd learnt about respect. Heather was simply attracting the wrong people into her life.

Assertiveness is often thought about in terms of the people we already know, and the relationships we're already in. However, assertiveness can be just as much about choosing who we will spend time with as it is about managing existing relationships.

Many people drift into relationships without a clear intention of what they want to give and gain from those relationships. They have high expectations and they make assumptions. Then they wonder why people let them down. 'Why did they treat me so badly?' they ask.

It's not so much that the person has purposely let them down; it's more likely that that person wasn't able to offer that level of regard and respect in the first place.

Why We Attract the Wrong People

It was clear that Heather had yet to learn the value of loving herself and creating her own sense of self-worth. She was so much in the habit of looking to others to validate her and make her feel good enough, that she didn't stop to consider if they were the right people or not. It made her relationships somewhat of a lottery!

There are various reasons why people attract the wrong people. Let's look at some of them.

Misplaced Empathy

We can attract the wrong people because of misplaced

empathy. As we saw in chapter 6 'Misplaced Empathy', in trying to be kind and considerate, we can overdo our good intentions—and end up drawing people into our lives who are in no position to offer us the regard and respect we deserve. If someone is hurt and suffering, it's not for us to rescue them—they need help in the context of a professional therapeutic relationship.

Beliefs About Deservedness

Sometimes people attract the wrong people simply because they don't think they deserve better. Often they aren't consciously aware of this—it's more likely an underlying limiting belief that's driving the way they think and the choices they make.

As we saw in Part 2 'Why Do We Find It So Hard to be Assertive', a belief is the conclusion we've come to, based on an event, or events, from the past. We take this conclusion and use it as a lens through which we view ourselves, others, and life in general. This is how we make up our mind about our own worth and what we deserve.

Heather told me about her growing up years. It was a lonely time. She'd had little connection with her brother, who was twenty-two years old and had already left home when she was born. Her parents made a living from buying and selling properties. Often, they would live in a property whilst it was being refurbished, doing much of the work themselves. Consequently, they moved a lot, and home was never a settled environment.

Moving from place to place, and often to a new school, Heather found it hard to make friends. Consequently, if anyone gave her the least bit of attention, she would jump at the chance to make a new friend. She didn't stop to assess what people were really like because she just didn't want to feel so alone. It became a pattern.

Attracting the Right People

Heather's low self-esteem meant that she had a habit of looking outwards to get validation and security. She didn't really have a sense of her own self-worth, or of the values that mattered to her. She just hadn't ever thought about it.

This is not unusual. Like Heather, many of the people I've helped over the years have been somewhat hazy when I ask them about their own values, and how they expect to be treated. Yet, gaining this self-awareness is key in leading a more confident and assertive life, because once you know who you are, and what you want from your relationships, you can start seeking that out in a more intentional way.

Think about it like this. If you joined a group of people with similar interests—let's use the example of say, photography—

you would meet like-minded people who are also interested in photography, so you would have a more meaningful connection with them. That's obvious.

However, we forget that this works on other levels too. Once you make clear your own values and guidelines, you'll more likely encounter people who share the same. However, there's no need to go around interviewing people! This is why I created the **Intentional Life Plan** for you, to help you get clarity on who you are and what you want. Complete the plan and you'll find that this simple act of being clear for yourself will help you to attract those people who are a good match for you. They'll begin to come into your awareness: you will notice them, and they will notice you.

Priming Your Mind

In every moment we're being bombarded with a great deal of sensory information—images, sounds, smells, etc. Imagine if we paid attention to all of it—we simply wouldn't be able to function in the world. So, there's a part of the brain called the Reticular Activating System (RAS), which filters the most important and relevant information for us and ignores the rest.

The good news is that we can actually *tell* the RAS what we consider to be relevant and important. It will then seek out that information and put our attention on it. You may have had a similar experience to the following example.

James was thinking about getting a new car. He decided he'd like a blue Ford Fiesta. Everywhere James went that week, he kept seeing blue Ford Fiestas.

In order to attract the right people into our lives then, we need to first decide what our values are. We then need to tell the RAS to start noticing people who have those values.

A really effective method to do this is to imagine you have already met a new person who is perfect for you. Whatever type of relationship you're seeking, imagine someone who treats you with regard and respect, who values themselves, and will value you too. In your mind, tell this new person what you enjoy about their company, what you admire about them and how much you appreciate them. In this way you are instructing your RAS to seek out these types of people and to present them to you in your everyday life.

A good way to make this even more effective is to write this person a letter. Put it in a safe place. Then, one day when they turn up in your life, you can show it to them!

What Comes Up for You When I Ask ... ?

I asked Heather the same question I've asked many clients:

'What comes up for you when I ask, '"Do you love yourself?"'

Like so many people had done before her, Heather paused for a moment, then tears came into her eyes.

'I don't know. I don't think I do, really.'

There's a common theme that I've noticed through helping people gain confidence. This is: they've been putting so much time and energy into seeking love and acceptance from others, that they've forgotten all about giving love and acceptance to themselves.

People seek validation from others in order to feel that they're good enough, likeable, and worthy. When they get this validation, it does bring them some sense of worthiness—they wouldn't do it otherwise—but this is often a short-lived *worthiness fix*. Very soon they're back to feeling insecure, and seeking approval again, because in their own minds they're judging, criticising and knocking their own confidence.

Of course, there's nothing wrong with seeking some approval from others; as we've seen, we all learn this *need to please* from a very early age. It's human nature to do so. To a point.

The problem is that if we keep expecting the greater part of our worthiness to come from the approval of other people, it becomes quite a gamble because they can't always be in a good space to provide it for us.

People lead busy lives. It's unrealistic, and actually unfair, to expect others to always be there with positive words and constant approval when they have their own life to focus on. They may be busy and distracted, and unable to offer the kindness and validation we crave in that moment in time.

It's far better then, to get into the good life habit of providing the greater part of love and acceptance for ourselves, and then rely on others for just an occasional kindly top-up!

A model I created for my clients is the **90/10 Percent Guideline for Self-Worth**. If you struggle with your confidence, it's very likely that you've been expecting 90 percent validation from others, and only offering yourself 10 percent, if even that. Once you start to flip that around, you'll find that your confidence rapidly increases. You can do this by placing much more emphasis on loving yourself.

You can get your copy of this guideline in the free companion course at the website

www.howkindpeople.com

Remember that your relationships will always reflect the relationship you have with yourself. The kinder you are to yourself, the more likely you will draw people into your life who will treat you with kindness, and the more easily you will be able to reciprocate their kindness. A loving, consciously kind and assertive win-win for all!

One Thing People Tend to Forget

I've noted that often when the subject of self-love comes up, the first thing a client will tell me is that they are paying attention to their diet, taking exercise, pampering themselves. This is what we call self-care. It is one very important part of self-love.

However, people tend to forget that self-love is also very much about how we talk to ourselves. While eating well and exercising will help you physically and mentally, you'll just keep getting knocked back if you're continually judging and criticising yourself.

Whenever you feel low, insecure, or lacking in confidence, know that that is the little child within. And as with any child, if you speak to them with judgement and criticism they won't flourish. On the other hand, if you speak to them with encouragement, validation, and approval, their confidence will soar.

So add in a good daily sprinkling of loving self-talk. Remind yourself that you are: worthy and lovable and doing just fine. I can tell you that this simple change of attitude and thinking works like magic. I've witnessed it in many, many clients. It has radically changed my life too!

Our Greatest Teachers

Every relationship, long or short, has value. Many of us have had one or two people in our lives who've caused us distress—people who have disregarded and disrespected us in some way. These people can have an intensely negative impact on our confidence. However, one way of looking at these people is to see them as great teachers in our lives. They teach us to be more self-aware, to remember our own self-worth and to seek out ways to assert ourselves.

It's a good idea, then, to look back on our times with these people not with regret, but with this question for each one: 'What can I learn from that experience?'

The very act of asking yourself this question means you are becoming more assertive, because it is courageous and self-loving to do so. It is about showing up as the authentic you—caring enough about yourself to want to learn and grow from every experience.

Attracting the right people into your life isn't about surrounding yourself with amazingly enlightened people who are faultless—none of us are perfect! We can all be lazy and distracted. Rather, it's about fundamental values. If we can find people who understand that it's important that we each aim to value our own worth, and that of others, then we're heading in the right direction.

Sum Up Points

- People put up with disrespect because they are not clear where they stand in relationships.
- Assertiveness can be just as much about choosing who we will spend time with in the future as it is about managing existing relationships.
- One way to attract the right people into your life is to treat yourself with love and respect.
- Some people do not have the insight and emotional intelligence required to treat us with respect and regard; it's unfair to try to demand that of them.
- Imagining the type of people you want to meet will prime your RAS to look out for them.
- Those people who treat us poorly can be our greatest teachers when we ask ourselves what we can learn from our experiences with them.

Self-Reflective Questions for How to Attract the Right People into Your Life

- What do I value most in my relationships?
- How can I treat myself with love and respect?
- What can I learn from my past challenging relationships?

In your **Intentional Life Plan,** you will find the template: **Attracting the Right People.** Consider these self-reflective questions and use your conclusions to help you complete it.

www.howkindpeople.com

Chapter 18
Your Exceptional Life

My lovely, and kind, reader, I'm so thrilled that we've been on this journey together. I hope that the guidance, tools, and the techniques in this book have been helpful to you.

Life is an ongoing journey into wisdom with constant new challenges and lessons to learn. You deserve to lead an exceptional life—a life of confidence, success, and great relationships. It's time for you to step into that life now.

Always remember:

Assertiveness begins in your heart space.

Be intentional and clear about what you want from your life and your relationships.

Be authentic, get to know yourself, and speak your truth.

Take courage and allow yourself to be vulnerable—it's OK.

Feel gratitude for this gift of life, so you'll want to make the most of it.

Speak to yourself in loving ways and treat yourself as you'd like others to treat you.

Be consciously kind to yourself and others, and seek solutions that create positive outcomes for all.

Take small steps; don't be hard on yourself. Remember that everyone finds it challenging to step into the light and be brave.

Remember that you are an evolving being, so enjoy this journey of life.

Complete your **Intentional Life Plan** and use it as your guide.

And so this book is coming to an end. It's been an honour and a privilege to share this special time with you. I wish for you so much happiness, so much confidence, and inspiring, fulfilling relationships.

Would you like to continue on this journey with me? **My Exceptional Life**, the membership, is an online programme where you can learn practical ways to apply the tools, tips, and techniques from this book—and more.

Plus, get access to a community where you can share your goals and achievements, find mutual support, and connect with like-minded people who want to lead an intentional, confident, and fulfilling life.

You can find out more about the **My Exceptional Life** membership programme at myexceptionallife.be

In Kindness

Marléne Rose Shaw

Thank you for reading *How Kind People Get Tough: Assertiveness Tools, Tips, and Techniques for More Confidence and Happier Relationships.*

If you enjoyed this book, please visit the site where you purchased it and write a brief review. Your feedback is important to me and will help other readers decide if they want to read the book too.

References

Chapter 1: Who Are the Kind People?

Chase, Michael J., *Am I Being Kind: how asking one simple question can change your life...and your world*, Hay House, 2011

Chapter 2: Can Kind People be Tough?

Harris, Thomas, *I'm Ok, You're Ok,* Harper Collins, 1967

Chapter 5: Limiting Beliefs
Shaw, Marléne Rose, *Out Of Fear Into Love: Life doesn't have to be a struggle*, Power of Love Books, 2016

Resources: Books

Chase, Michael J *Am I Being Kind: how asking one simple question can change your life...and your world*, Hay House, 2011

Harris, Thomas, *I'm Ok, You're Ok,* Harper Collins, 1967

Shaw, Marléne Rose, *Out Of Fear Into Love: Life doesn't have to be a struggle,* Power of Love Books, 2016

Craig, Gary, *The EFT Manual*, Elite Books, 2011

Resources: Websites

How Kind People - Resources for this book
www.howkindpeople.com

Founder of EFT, Gary Craig
www.emofree.com

EFT International

https://eftinternational.org/

Hay House
www.hayhouse.co.uk

Marléne Rose Shaw
wwwmarleneroseshaw.com

My Exceptional Life membership
myexceptionallife.be

About the Author

Marléne Rose Shaw is a therapist, coach and self-help author. Over the past 25 years, she has been privileged to help thousands of people.

She loves to teach people simple and actionable steps to help them make rapid shifts towards more confidence, overcoming anxiety, and happier relationships.

Contact Details:

For one-to-one sessions via Skype or at my practice:

www.marleneroseshaw.com

Facebook:
facebook.com/CounsellingAndTherapyMShaw

Instagram:
instagram.com/marleneroseshaw

Twitter:
twitter.com/MarleneRoseShaw

Printed by Amazon Italia Logistica S.r.l.
Torrazza Piemonte (TO), Italy

17018644R00153